THE OPTIONAL GOD

THE
OPTIONAL GOD

STEPHEN F. BAYNE, Jr.
Bishop of Olympia

New York · OXFORD UNIVERSITY PRESS

1953

For
BURTON SCOTT EASTON
and
FRANK GAVIN

FOREWORD

THERE is a belief, held commonly enough in our world, that the religious issue — the question of the reality of God — is a side issue. We do not readily deny God's existence (at least Western man does not); but we look at the possibility of God as at best a helpful supplement to the real dynamics of life. It makes no fundamental difference whether He exists or not. It is useful to Western society to believe in Him, and such belief is to be commended; on the other hand, the basic activities of our democracies must be constructed to get along without Him. In the words I use as a title, God is optional.

This book is an attempt to express that theory, and to look at its implications in four of the cardinal areas of life. I am, of course, looking at those implications from the point of view of the Church, and as a Churchman. It would be idle for me, as it would be for anyone, to pretend to neutrality; I am not neutral; I feel that the myth of the optional God is untrue and destructive and highly dangerous to the fabric of our civilization. But I am uncomfortable at the suggestion that the secular world is simply to be damned for believing the myth. The question is far more complicated than that, and the response of the Church must be far more radical than we generally are willing to admit. I have tried to sketch, at least briefly, something of what that response should be, and in the last chapter to give a coherent, Christian view of the universe, in which, as I see it, is hidden the only possible basis for believing in a universe at all.

It may perhaps help to place this book in some perspective to say that it is based on the Bishop Paddock Lectures, given by myself to the faculty and students of the General Theological Seminary in New York City, in February 1952. That foundation is an honored one, which in the past has been adorned by as great a Christian thinker as William Temple; and I count it a most generous privilege to have been invited to give these lectures.

I must acknowledge with gratitude the kindness of the Educational Policies Commission of the National Education Association for permission to quote from its publication *Moral and Spiritual Values in the Public Schools;* of Harcourt, Brace and Company for permission to quote from *Abraham Lincoln: The Prairie Years,* by Carl Sandburg, and from *The Rock,* by T. S. Eliot; of the Newman Press for permission to quote from *Revolution in a City Parish,* by Abbe G. Michonneau; of the Student Christian Movement Press for permission to quote from *Work in Modern Society,* by J. H. Oldham; and of the Yale University Press for permission to quote from *Horace Mann and Religion in the Massachusetts Public Schools,* by Raymond D. Culver.

I want also, particularly, to mention three teachers

from whom, in various ways, I have gained great light. Charles Norris Cochrane and William Aylott Orton have both gone on ahead of us; I must own myself endlessly grateful to both for profound scholarship and unique and sensitive imagination. The third, Peter F. Drucker, has taught me a great deal over all the years since I first read *The Future of Industrial Man*. I hardly need say that I do not burden any of these men with responsibility for my thoughts or conclusions (except that anybody who writes a book gives a hostage to preachers). What I say, I say on my own; but I would not have said it if I had not read and been moved and encouraged by what these men have written, and I am most grateful to them.

Finally, I think it is fair to say about this book that it is the writing of an unashamed liberal in what is now generally called the 'old-fashioned' sense of the term. It is not a comfortable philosophy in a world of snarling absolutisms, but this would trouble me more if I were not so sure that true liberalism is nothing but the even temper of a man to whom God is not optional.

STEPHEN F. BAYNE, JR.

The Bishop's House
Seattle, Washington
May 1953

CONTENTS

THE OPTIONAL GOD

I

THE OPTIONAL GOD

PERIODICALLY the Church rediscovers the first century. My generation did so; we came into consciousness after the First World War, during the years when the old, spacious optimism — the easy, nineteenth-century comfortableness about life and the world — was collapsing. We were a 'lost generation,' not actually in the picturesque way we liked to imagine ourselves, dramatically facing Doomsday with a pleasant alcoholic eschatology, but lost because we needed to find a new frame of reference within which we could understand what was happening around us.

Many of us within the Christian body found such a framework in the discovery of the peculiar and inviting parallelism between the world of the twentieth century and the world of the first century. My own memory in this respect runs back more than twenty years to a casual remark made by a preacher to a congregation of divinity students, myself among them. I do not remember even who he was but, as if it were yesterday, I remember his speaking of the infinite remoteness, to our minds, of the issues and attitudes of the Renaissance and the Reformation, in contrast to the vivid familiarity of the climate of the New Testament — its people and their choices and problems. 'We are infinitely closer to the first century than we are to the sixteenth' — he used some such phrase as that, and to me, suddenly, the aimless and opaque misery of my world in transition fitted into a scheme I could understand. If the world of the New Testament could explain and illuminate my world, then I could identify what I wanted to fight and what I was fighting for, and the pain of the times, like birth pains, could point to a deliverance.

Like all commonplaces, the remark is an oversimplification and leads, as I have come to think, to dangerous misreadings. But for me it had great catalytic value at the time; and even though the remark requires the most profound qualification, still it precipitated and crystallized understanding for a whole generation of us and gave us a perspective within which we could set and see the mission of the Church in our time.

Indeed it was not too long before we were to see, especially in European Christianity under the flail of totalitarianism and war, a sharp and quite self-conscious return to the world of the New Testament. Both in the Confessional bodies and in the Roman Church how clearly the first-century frame of reference has emerged, as in the heroic constancy of Bishop Berggrav or the compelling apostolate of Abbe Michonneau.

The world has a first-century 'feel' to it; the comparison of that century with our own presents an unmistakable and most inviting parable; and a whole generation has been both helped and harmed by it.

We have been helped because so much of the true nature and mission of Christianity is clearer and sharper against the background of the first century. We have been harmed because the men of the twentieth century and their minds are so different from those of nineteen centuries ago.

We need not have been surprised by the ambivalence of the parable. The reading of history is like a play; a great play illuminates, vivifies, teaches, objectifies — but it ends, and the lights go up, and we have no right to feel cheated because we must leave the magic and go home to a different place and to issues less clear and speeches less well managed.

But how it has helped all of us to learn more of the world of the first century and to examine the Gospel against that background. For instance, there is the remarkable way in which we have understood afresh the true nature of Christian initiation. Holy Baptism and Confirmation have, in one generation, regained an ancient clarity in our eyes. The Christian Community, especially gathered at the Lord's Table, has come again to the center of our gaze. Our preaching has reclaimed a forgotten power as we have come anew to sense the hopelessness of men without God in the world.

In all this process of rediscovery, which indeed is to me the most notable theological development in these last years, we have been immeasurably helped by the parable of the first century.

We have been helped, too, in our understanding of the events and forces in our own history. The 'failure of nerve' which Bury observed in the ancient world seems astonishingly contemporary. The defensiveness and the ossification of Rome in the early Christian time seem to reappear in the homesickness and fearfulness of the West in our time. It is easier to understand the McCarran Act when we have read first-century Roman legislation, and easier to evaluate the panicky question 'Are you now or have you ever been a member of the Communist Party?' when we remember older inquisitors and an older question, 'Are you a Christian?' The barbarians glared across the frontiers then much as they do now; and the all-powerful State came more and more to find welcome as the guardian of order and peace, as indeed it does to many in our day. The bankruptcy of classic philosophy finds a parallel in the empty and arid scholasticism of scientific naturalism in a twentieth-century classroom.

All these likenesses have their uses. But as we are tempted to draw them out, so do we begin uncomfortably to see that a parable is not an allegory — it is not a map or a chart or a blueprint. A parable, like a star shell, is expected to go off and give a brilliant light for a little while so we can get our bearings. It is like the lance which kills a whale — it slices painlessly and unnoticed through the blubber, and then the explosive head detonates to the fatal discomfiture of the whale. But the lance was not intended to tell the whale where to swim next. The Pharisees and scribes got precious few rules for daily living from the story of the lost sheep. Indeed, it is the way of the Pharisee to waste his time speculating on who the lost sheep are; and it is our way to wonder idly how we shall identify the twentieth-century barbarian or Nero or Cicero or Paul, and there are none, really, except in our own hearts.

I am merely saying that historical parables mislead as well as help. As we have been strengthened and cleansed by a recovery of the sense of crisis and conflict which dominates the New Testament, so have we been beguiled and our judgment dulled by our attempt to identify the characters in that ancient drama with our own men and movements.

We have been misled because, of all the Christian certainties about history, none is surer than that history does not repeat itself. Time is as real as the Incarnation; we are not trapped in an endless cycle; there is a beginning and an end to history; and therefore there is nothing under the sun that happens over again. Men live, and choose, and die; and if we say that nations and civilizations in a measure also must choose and die, it is still, as with men, that the time is always new and the choice is fresh and the protagonists are strangers in every age. God does not let us easily avoid our choices by the fiction that this has all happened before and we have only to wait out the inevitable. Our history will be nothing else but the fabric of our own freedom, or lack of it.

More than this, such a mood of retreat to history can often nourish a destructive and illusory retirement from life — it can appeal to the defensive and timid and self-regarding in us, and appear to justify failure and indecision. 'Back to the catacombs' is a useful and healthy slogan, as long as it signifies a fresh return to first principles. But how dangerous a slogan it can be to the doctrinaire little parson who by it seeks to defend his failure or refusal to cope with his own problems and those of his congregation. He does not like the difficult, uneasy apostolate to a secularized generation; he has not enough love or patience or skill to preach the Gospel to the people committed to his care; and, under cover of the first century, he retreats into a catacomb more real than he imagines and plays at being a first-century Christian, complete with persecution (by unsympathetic laymen), with candles in the early dawn, and with the faithful women.

It is a very dangerous mood, it seems to me — this 'back-to-the-catacombs, back-to-the-first-century' mood. When the Church yields to it, we are likely to see things in false perspective, to interpret as 'paganism' or 'persecution' what is no more than an honest evaluation of what we preach, or to mistake archeology for primitive purity. The parable misleads when we seek the appearance of it, when hurt pride is mistaken for apostolic Christianity, or when personal eccentricity, liturgical or otherwise, tries to mask itself as a 'return to the Gospel.'

All this is obvious enough; and so is the root difficulty of all — the parable misleads most when it leads us to forget that most important fact, that *we live in a post-Christian age.*

Because of the inheritance of centuries of faith, which has endowed our words and institutions with significances that persist even though half-forgotten and irrelevant, much of the sharpness and clarity of the issues in first-century Christianity are precisely what is absent from the battlefield of the twentieth century. It is a battlefield, and we must not underestimate it; yet each time I read *Alice in Wonderland* I think the account of the croquet game is one of the best images I know of the exasperating task of the preacher in our time. You remember that nightmare game — with the wickets moving around to get directly in front of the Queen, and the balls unrolling and walking off just as the players prepare to hit them, and even the mallets, the flamingoes, bending their necks to look soulfully upward as the players begin their swings.

Trying to preach the Gospel is no less infuriating than that. The goal is never quite where you think it is going to be; you start off after the profit motive, say, or nationalism, and the first thing you know you are aiming directly at Christian morality. You take a swing at the ball — at covetousness, say, or gluttony — and suddenly it turns out to be the last church bazaar you attended or the recent meeting of your main woman's organization. Even your weapon will not stay passive and firm in your hands; it writhes around as you smite, and you find yourself looking into the stern and

admonitory eyes of your once-favorite theologian or
the House of Bishops or a new and confusing transla-
tion of the Bible.

All of which is only to say that the battlefield of the
Gospel in our time is not nearly as clear as we should
like it, or as the New Testament pictures it. Enemies
turn out to be friends; old allies become bitter enemies; ancient issues suddenly seem of little importance; we forget what we are fighting for; new causes
deflect and interrupt us. This is the peculiar problem
of Christianity in a post-Christian world. Paganism
with Christian words and Christian values is quite a
different enemy, and a far more difficult one to identify, than its first-century counterpart. The State that
has been nourished and clothed with Christian ideas
presents a problem radically different from the decayed
mass of impersonal rights and penalties confronting
the first Christians. Our words are ambiguous ones —
'personality,' 'love,' 'community,' 'history,' 'science'
carry long-forgotten theological inflections which now
confuse as often as they reveal. The overtones of our
duties to our neighbors are, by inheritance, often
Christian ones; yet the duties themselves now are so
often circumscribed by secularism that they are impossible of Christian fulfillment, even of Christian understanding. We use, and with sincerity, the very word
'Christian' as an adjective to describe such massive
and complex phenomena as education, civilization,
culture, signifying by it what may actually be no more
than conventional or inherited standards; yet even in

this use of 'Christian' there is still a dim consciousness that in the background there lies a belief which was once all-important even though now it is forgotten.

It is a tangled, confused battle we fight, all the more so because the war extends even within our own ranks. It is a civil war, the cruelest and most costly that man can ever fight. For, as the outlines of Christian faith have been smudged and blurred in the world outside, all too often have they been equally confused within the Christian family.

It is inviting to say that we should put our own house in order first, as if there were a temporal priority in these matters. Actually the war is a single one, as it has always been; the battle ranges freely over both a distant field and within the known household of faith with equal force; the redemption of a post-Christian world is vitally and immediately connected with the redemption of a post-Christian Church. If, as you read these pages, I seem to say more about the world than the Church, it is not that I forget the Body which I serve; it is rather that the witness we bear in the world more often than not is a two-edged sword.

One reason I have said all this is to remind myself — and you too, if you need reminding — that in any analysis we make of the mission and vocation of the Church in our secular world we must begin with the postulate that our secularism is a post-Christian secularism.

Our first impulse is to say that it makes no difference. Secularism is universal; it suffers no adjectives; 'a world organized as if there were no God,' which is a handy definition of the secular world, cares not at all what God it ignores.

I make two comments. One is that I think a more exact definition of the secular world, at least our world, is 'a world organized as if it made no difference whether there were a God or no.' Our world is very far from ready to act on the assumption that there is no God. We are at once too cautious, too nostalgic, and too indecisive to accept the logic of atheism as baldly as that. Moreover, we think we have found a way to play both ends against the middle, to hedge the immemorial bet of faith. We prefer to organize our lives as if it made no difference whether there be a God or no. Thus those who choose belief may have it, with whatever advantage it brings. Those who do not so choose are at least at no disadvantage. Thus all win, and all have prizes, to quote *Alice* again.

But one of the conditions of this compromise is that we shall all, or mostly all, accept a basic common stock of agreed values. In the West this agreed tradition is still what is called 'Christian.' One of the results of this unspoken compact within society has been the appearance, on a major scale, of the typical post-Christian, secular man. He is legion. In effect you do not at all disturb him by questioning his religious or Christian belief. He may indeed tell you himself — or his relatives and relicts will certainly tell you — that he never was a churchgoer but he surely was a good, Christian man if ever there was one. He has, this typical man, arrived at the essential discrimination in our peculiar secular adventure. That is to say, he may not adhere too closely to the historic Christian beliefs, but he must not, and his relatives must attest to it, concede that his practical rules of life are anything but Christian, of purest ray serene.

This is not altogether hypocrisy; indeed it rises, as I shall presently show, to a sublime height in a great soul. Much of this profession of Christian standards is poppycock; but, poppycock or no, it is usually sincere, and in point of fact the level of life the secular man achieves is commonly as high as that of his churchgoing brother.

What is important is that he still feels it necessary to support and defend the tradition he inherits. Even though he agrees that it makes no difference whether there be a God, still it is the Christian God who is so importantly unimportant. He usually cannot give you a good reason why he adheres to the ethical code born out of an optional faith. He often has nothing but panicky repression with which to meet the advance of a different code springing from a different and living faith. He may try to justify his inherited attitudes and habits by stumbling and stammering that they are 'good business,' or he may have some wretched jargon of 'service' or psychology with which to excuse his adherence to them. But at heart he is bound by ties stronger than he knows. The ties are in his bloodstream; they are in his dim memory of heroic choices long past; like the sea calling us all, fascinating and frightening because it is the mother of waters from which we came, so is the inherited faith of a post-Christian age in the mind and heart of an ordinary child of that age.

In the extraordinary child — in the great soul — the same tensions and discriminations are at work, often at a sublime level. Mrs. Lincoln said about her husband once, 'He never joined a church, but still he was a religious man. But it was a kind of poetry in his nature, and he never was a technical Christian.' * It hardly needs saying that Lincoln was worlds away from accepting the dogma of the optional God. Indeed there was a nobility and passion in his belief which was as close to the prophetic level as that of any man we shall ever know. Yet in even so great a soul we can see the same strain and pressure toward the division of faith from morals.

Dilute a Lincoln with four generations of religious neutrality; smother the fires of his spirit with ninety years of fat living; plaster his roughness over with partisan idolatry; stamp out the texture and individuality of the frontier man; and what is left is the fragmentary unbeliever whose 'Christianity' is little more than polite conformity.

In truth I think Abraham Lincoln is the archetype of the most stubborn problem with which an American preacher has to cope. There was the time, during his first campaign for the presidency, when he was apprais-

* Carl Sandburg, *Abraham Lincoln: The Prairie Years,* New York, Harcourt, Brace and Co., 1926, p. 278.

ing the support of churches and churchmen in Springfield and commented sadly to a friend, 'Here are 23 ministers of different denominations, and all of them are against me but three.' Then, with tears glistening on his face, 'I know there is a God, and that He hates injustice and slavery. I see the storm coming, and I know that His hand is in it. If He has a place and work for me I believe I am ready. I am nothing but truth is everything . . . I may not see the end; but it will come, and I shall be vindicated; *and these men will find they have not read their Bibles aright.'* * This from the man who 'never was a technical Christian'!

That terrible charge was a righteous judgment on the trivial and fearful congregations of which Lincoln spoke. That is in part what I mean by saying that he is a problem to preachers. But I would also bid you see, in its noblest and most generous expression, the swift, strong current of the knowledge of good and evil which runs out from under the ice of a frozen and dead faith in a post-Christian, secular society. By imperceptible steps, men move from the vision of God first to an impatience with those who claim to know God and who do not really see or hear Him at all; then to a resolution, wise or foolish, to keep what they do know and can claim for themselves; then, finally, to a practical certainty that the God is optional, and that all that really matters is the life, which, long ago, was born in faithful discipleship.

* *Abraham Lincoln: The Prairie Years,* pp. 372–3 (italics mine).

But the name is important, at least in our time. It is a post-Christian secularism.

The second comment I make on the phrase 'post-Christian' is this: words matter. The tools — the words — we use in this world of the optional God are tools that still bear the Christian form and fit the Christian sizes. It is more than a semantic problem. 'Democracy' may, and does, have one meaning with us in America, and a slightly different one in England, and a grotesquely different one in Russia. That is a semantic problem, I suppose, in part. But those same words — 'democracy,' 'freedom,' 'individuality,' 'man,' 'society,' the indispensable words in our tradition — present a unique problem to the twentieth-century man, Christian or not, who proposes to use them. They are not negative or neutral counters that will fit any system. They are ambiguous; they involve meanings and choices that often confuse issues and darken counsel; they presuppose beliefs no longer understood; they are too big for secular man alone for they assume a stature in man which, without God, he does not have. So he rattles around inside words several sizes too large, and he is increasingly involved in this more-than-semantic problem.

We are somewhat at the stage of a dinner party of experts, if you can imagine such a calamity, where the philosopher and the plumber and the physicist must spend all their time defining the terms they propose to use, where the neo-orthodox parson is off in a corner talking with his fingers, and the professional educator flees to the pantry to engage in a democratic experience with the help.

If you think this is a ridiculous caricature, then I urge you to attend carefully a typical session in pre-marital counseling, say. As enjoined by the canons, the clergyman sets aside a time to prepare his parish children for marriage. He discusses the meaning of the word 'love,' which appears in the marriage ritual and figures prominently in the general marital picture.

Because he has been instructed himself, he knows that the word 'love' means something you do rather than something you feel. He is aware that no man, however free, could take so grave a vow as to feel loving toward his wife till death do them part. He is aware, however, that the heart of the Christian life is contained in the profound assertion that man is free to bind himself, with God's help, to a faithful and gentle partnership with another free soul — in short, that man is master of himself, under God; that he is in charge of things generally; and that his freedom rises to its highest pitch in his free self-giving in loyal honor to his wife. 'Love' is, then, something a man does — a word that describes the greatest freedom, born out of a cold and disciplined will, nourished with the love of the eternal Father.

The two candidates, mercifully, are so much in love with each other that they are anaesthetized for all practical purposes. Usually only after six months or so do they remember what was said to them, after the first rapture has gone, and they awaken to discover that they are still, in the main, the same persons they were before, and they begin the slow, arduous, wonderful task of giving themselves, choice by choice, each to the other. Only then do they begin to face the stubborn fact of meaning.

To them love was a swift, sweet wind which swept them tumultuously out of their privacies into a common life. To her, perhaps, it meant a breathless self-giving; to him, a manly assumption of a new dignity and a more sober bearing in the world. Perhaps to one the word signified the passionate hunger to give and to take; to the other a certain right to happiness and an inner security, careless and profound.

But the real discovery of marriage is that 'love' means, first of all, not a sensation, or a gift, or a part you play, but a steady resolution of the will, the finest act of a free man. If the word means that to children as they learn it, then half the battle of marriage is already won. If the word does not mean that, if the overtones be lost or only dimly remembered through some surrogate, then the whole Christian understanding of marriage is imperiled, and the promises at the altar are either sentimentally accepted or said simply as a part of 'the traditional beauty of the (Episcopal) service,' and the very dream itself is lost.

And if the dream be lost, then the fact is lost. The destructive, corrosive solvent of marriage in our time is not weakness or failure in the human material. We are not any worse in those respects than our fathers were. What is wrong at the heart of marriage is that we do not understand what the words mean. We use them freely, yet we have forgotten the sense of them; and the whole magnificent, incredible ideal of Christian marriage perishes because we no longer understand what we are promising or believe that it is possible.

Words matter, precisely because they are not neutral signs or counters but come to us still warm from the living hands that have formed them, artifacts of a size and shape to fit the use — the dream, the hope, the choice, the faith, the audacity — that calls them into being. They are like hormones of the spirit to us, awakening and stirring into growth the ultimate potentialities of the spirit. They are decidedly not neutral, nor are they susceptible to whatever meaning a given age wishes to assign to them.

This is particularly important to say when we are thinking about the pivotal words of our society, such as the ones I cite — 'freedom,' 'man,' 'individuality,' 'personality,' and the rest. Those are the words on which our life rests, by and large. They are words whose meanings and dimensions were enormously expanded by Christian use and Christian understanding. Trace back any one of them through the exciting years when they came into our language, when the advancing frontiers of faith required of us tools big enough for the breaking of the new ground of the spirit. Then contrast the mood of that society, eager and ardent in the search for words big enough to express what it felt about the size and destiny of man, with the mood of a society like our own, contracting and shrinking, feeling no need for such great words because it has no such great beliefs, yet still obliged to use them for it cannot and dare not go backward. The contrast of those moods illustrates, as for example the use of the word 'love,' why the qualification 'post-Christian' is an essential one.

The God Whom we ignore, the optional God, is the Christian God. The words are still the Christian words. The moral habits, the ethical questions, the political improvisations are still, in general terms, those nourished by Christian faith. This is what I mean by 'post-Christian,' of course, and it is this condition that affects so profoundly the Christian assault on secularism in our world.

Let me comment, finally, on two factors that bear directly on the Mission of the Church in this post-Christian society of ours.

One is external; it is the progressive limitation of function that has more and more stultified the Church by 'professionalizing' it. If God be optional, then the aims and interests of the Church must be optional too, as far as they relate to God. I mean no very subtle change here; we have all seen it and commented on it. Little by little, the affairs of human society, education, social welfare, et cetera, have been separated from the Church's supposed field of interest. Economics has ceased to be regarded as a field of moral theology; politics loses more and more of its root relation to ethics. Little by little, as the implications of the theory of the optional God become plain, the place of the Church, of religion, in life is adjusted accordingly.

Increasingly the Church is expected to devote itself to something called 'religion.' The minister of religion is tolerated — indeed welcomed — as a coadjutor. In social casework, for example, it is conceded that in ministering to religious people it is often helpful to have a clergyman in the picture to bolster and interpret the solution worked out by the social worker. Or, in another example, the help of the Church is often sought in the fight against Communism or in the defense of free enterprise. That help is not essential; but it is good and positive; and in many ways the free enterprise system invites it.

But the help is assumed to be what is called 'religious.' In the casework problem what is at stake is not a Christian view of personality; it is rather the using of religion as an instrument to help the client adjust to and understand a secular solution. An optional God is not an end in Himself — He exists (if He exists) to lend His strength to the secular solution. Religion is a means, regarded as potentially helpful to many good causes.

I doubt whether religion is really helpful to the secular society; I rather think it will be the death of that society in the end; but, in our time at least, the Church has a precarious, specialized, professionalized hold on a place in society. We are the chaplains of the *status quo*, a pleasant career for idealistic and bookish men who are able to adapt well to the mores of their post-Christian friends.

The difficulty of being purely 'religious' is one familiar to the clergy. It really takes enormous skill to preach a whole sermon and not say anything about anything except 'religion.' We have the greatest admiration for the dexterity of those who can do it. But, difficult as it is, to many of our friends and well-wishers it is still the role to assign to us — we are assumed to be the experts in charge of the 'religious department' of the outfit. It is not a very basic department; it is comparable, say, to 'imported chinaware' or 'chauffeur's uniforms' in a modern department store. But, for whatever it is worth, there it is; and as a business friend said to me not long ago, in protest against the socialistic preaching of some of our clergy, 'The free-enterprise system has made a big place for the Church in American life, and the Church had better play ball or they will lose it.'

The second factor is internal; it is the more-or-less deliberate acceptance by the Church of the role assigned to it in our society. The man whose comment I just quoted is a churchman, if a somewhat tentative one; he accepts the fiction that the Church's interest really is in this wispy and unsubstantial thing called 'religion.' The tragedy is that he may well have learned the fiction from comfortable and 'religious' sermons by acquiescent and contented clergymen who would agree not only with the fact of the tolerance of the Church by free enterprise, which nobody would argue with anyway, but also with the profoundly false theory underlying it. A Church that has accepted the dogma of the optional God is a Church that has abdicated its mission to human society; it has no mission; it has only a seat in the secular train, at clergy rates, which apply only to the slower trains.

A curious consequence of this is that the more purely 'religious' we become — the more of the world we leave out of the Church — the easier it is to leave out God too. How many sermons there are preached, Sunday by Sunday, from which every mention of God could be subtracted without doing any appreciable damage to the sermon at all. Erase 'God' and substitute any one of a variety of surrogates — 'a peaceful society,' 'emotional adjustment,' 'the democratic way of life,' 'American ideals' — the result would be the same, and the encouraged self-approval of the parishioners would be unchanged.

The optional God can be dispensed with inside a secularized Church quite as well as outside. Certain linguistic problems are awkward, no doubt; but if you never preach on the doctrine of God, and use Him as an adjective as often as possible, even these are solved. The edges are blurred, and your chaplaincy to the secular world is secure.

I speak harshly; I hope it will not be forgotten that I speak principally of the Church I know, and incidentally love and try to serve, and that I speak also autobiographically. Anglicanism is often the chief offender in this complacent surrender. More at home in the world than other companies of Christian people, we are too often of the world, too. I used to fear for the future of the Episcopal Church; I do so no longer; it will never die. If it did not exist it would have to be invented; in any society, the religion of respectable self-congratulation is essential, and whatever Church captures that interest is secure forever. It can adapt itself readily to any society, able always to defend itself by the supple magic of its history and tradition from any charge of faithlessness, able always to be comfortable in any climate with its well-known breadth and inclusiveness. 'The Episcopal Church is the most comfortable of all churches because it interferes the least with a man's religion.' That is the common jibe; and it is too often true of us at our worst. To some degree, however, this is not a uniquely Anglican failing but rather the common failing of contemporary Christendom expressed in Anglican terms.

In our bad moods we develop the 'painless' irrelevances — such as the 'painless Catholicism' of our Anglican family. Have we not all the Catholic gifts? Have we not priests and altars and the historic sacraments and the ancient order and discipline of the Catholic Church? Of course we have, and in the most convenient form. We have the Eucharist, and we can tuck it away comfortably at an early hour so it will not offend those who like 'the regular service.' We have Confession, but it is never mandatory and is performed in a cultured and scientific manner. We have this and that — all extremely valuable as polemic weapons. Our arguments against the Roman claims are invincible; there is no question about our fully Catholic equipment and organization.

But how heart-breaking it is, this painless and theoretical Catholicism of the unattended altar and the cold and empty church. A Catholicism that is no more than an historical argument is worthless. It is only a piquant and picturesque form of optional religion, slightly more decorative than most. How the newspapers love, or try to love, 'the traditional and colorful procession of the clergy' in stoles and hoods at a high-grade ecclesiastical orgy. Picturesque and historic, indeed, but also quite irrelevant. What is actually talked about and taught and practiced may be no incandescent flame of the supernatural life at all; it may be only the private, irrelevant, professionalized language of technical 'religion' dressed in a theoretical Catholicism.

We need to be reminded, as William Temple reminded us, that 'It is a great mistake to suppose that God is only, or even chiefly, concerned with religion.' * Yet the world makes that supposition of the optional God, and the Church sometimes acquiesces in it and is infected by it, and the result is the 'painless Catholicism,' or its Protestant equivalent, which is equally hateful to God. Barren ritual and empty and theoretical historicity have their counterpart in a 'Protestantism' that means no more than that a man does not have to go to Church much, or believe very much, as

* William Temple, *The Hope of a New World*, London, S.C.M. Press, 1940, p. 70.

long as he votes against the Roman Church. In England I believe such persons sign themselves as 'C. of E.' In our country the parallel is any one of a dozen interesting misspellings familiar to all military chaplains. For example, 'prosdunt,' 'Prostent' and 'Babdist' are three that linger in my memory.

Here I have discussed chiefly my own Church, because I know it best. Yet I think it would be fair to say that, in different ways perhaps, every Christian body shows the signs of the optional God, the conventionalities, the irrelevances. Anglicanism develops in her peculiar historical way, with her vestigial prelatism which we all love as long as it is not taken too seriously. But there are other variations. The fringe sects, the charismatics, have their variety of irrelevance — the retreat into the Apocalypse or into the Epistle to the Romans. The sublime irrelevance of neo-orthodoxy is of a piece with this, in part; it need not be, but it often is no more than a pleasant exercise in word-spinning for the initiate. Great segments of both Protestant and Catholic thought now practically identify the Gospel and a liberal-Republican interpretation of the free-enterprise system, to the advantage of neither. Often, too, in the deep resurgence of interest in liturgical worship and its revival, there is hidden what amounts to a substitution of a form of service for a vital and immediate certainty of Divine action and Divine love. We are all in the same boat, in this; for all parts of the Christian community alike feel the impact of the dogma of the optional God; and all alike face the

danger of believing that dogma and accepting the sub-
ordinate and specialized 'religious' role assigned to the
Church by society.

This is the heart of the problem of the Church's mission to society, in this year of grace. It is a society dominated by a myth — that the question of God is a secondary question. That myth has an effect on the
Church as destructive as its effect on the State, the
school, industry . . . indeed everything in our lives.
Is the answer to the myth of Optionalism simply to
damn secular society as 'bad' — to say that it is an
enemy and that the Church's job is to destroy it or flee
from it?

The pages which follow are, in part, an attempt to
answer that question. But I would say this — that the
answer is written not chiefly in books or lectures, but in
the faces of men. The critic who is quick to condemn
the shallowness and the vulgarity, the emptiness and
hopelessness of a secular society — even the honest
critic who seeks to understand the riddle — will do
well to walk much in the streets of the city. He will
know how great are the gifts that Christian faith has
made to modern society; he will remember and use the
words still lambent with Christian meanings; he will
accept and understand the institutions around him —
the civil liberties, the assumptions of democracy, the
granite foundations of the meaning and dignity of man
that still support the weight of the whole grand structure of our society. All this he will thoughtfully and
gratefully receive as the legacy of faith. He will under-

stand that ours is, in the phrase, a 'post-Christian society,' living on inherited wealth.

But he will know more. He will look at the men around him; there he will see the scars of history. From them he will hear the accents of other tongues, and his mind will take him back to old oppression and ancient cruelty. He will look at them and understand that the Church has been, to many, not a blessing but a curse. He will understand the rejection of a Church that 'has not read its Bible aright.' He will see men turn away from a Church that seems concerned only for its own perpetuation as an institution. He will come to see something of the circularity of the Church, seeming so often to exist simply for the sake of existing. He will remember the fat callousness of clericalism, and how the sins of the fathers are visited on the children. He will remember the ghetto, and the slave ships, and all the endless misery of Christian man's inhumanity to man. He will understand that the Cross has meant privilege and hardness of heart as often as it has meant light and healing.

These things will not be simply historical data to him. He will see them live in a gesture or a word, in a sneer or a doubt. And he will understand that a secular society is, first of all, Judgment; and that the first mission of the Church is to understand Judgment and live up to it. To the critic God is not optional; he knows that God reigns, and that he 'shaves with a hired razor.' Therefore the critic walks the streets in penitence.

Penitence and pity; for he understands what this

free society has meant as hope and opportunity to the hopeless the world around. So pity is part of it; and a greater humility, for he sees, too, that the core of past misery more often than not has been ignorance and blindness and hardness of heart on the part of those who had power and did not use it aright, who had humility and forgot it.

And finally he comes to see the immense promise that has gleamed and beckoned to so many in the great secular experiment. He will know that the promise is not possible without God. He will know that the dreams of science and freedom could not be dreamed except for the sober daylight of God who makes knowledge possible. But yet he will exult in what knowledge and freedom there is, because it can lead back to God as surely as it came from Him.

Knowing these things, seeing them in the faces of men, the critic will also remember One Who told him long ago about the Light and the Leaven. It was not a comfortable, complacent world that was promised, nor a world that was to be safe for Christianity. It was not peace but a sword that was promised — not obedience and docility and conformity, but the life-giving restlessness of the yeast.

Remembering those far-off words, and the faces of his brothers seeking, as men have always sought, for a little more light and a more certain hope, the critic will turn to the Church again. He will not have any easy generalizations about what the twenty-first century will look like. He will know little more than what our

Lord gave the Church at the beginning — a comrade-ship and a flame and a table. He will know that there is no perfect society — that we have here no abiding city, but only the glorious and endless struggle to speak and live the truth as we see it. He will know that in the intense comradeship of the Water and the Bread and Wine there is still hidden the hope of the world. He will know that honest and courageous witness, and the life lived and shared at the center, are all God requires; the event is in the hands of God. And he will be content. 'The disciple is not above his master.'

II

COMMUNITY AND COMMUNION

LIKE MOST Americans, the least useful or adequate part of my education has been in the field of political theory and history. It is a basic defect, stemming in part from the disappearance of classical studies, and in part, I suppose, from the self-satisfaction of a successful and enclosed civilization like our own. Until very recent times we had only fragmentary knowledge of political systems or theories other than the comfortable one we enjoyed; our outlook was intensely insular; our major experience in conflicting political theories lay a century or more behind us, smugly wrapped in the mythology of the bad English king and the stuffy prelates and the wicked redcoats and the glorious victory that made us the best and happiest of people.

There has never been a people, I think, as gullible to such mythology as ourselves, or as badly prepared to face the decisive conflicts that now approach us, indeed now engage us. We need the balance and perspective that classical studies would have given us, and the experience the imperial adventure gave our English and

Continental kinsmen. But we have neither; and the
lack will be costly to us in the end.

I am aware of this inadequacy whenever I try to state
clearly what the mission of the Church is in the face of
the twentieth-century State. Neither historical nor
theoretical inquiry helps very much except perhaps to
encourage and bolster our instincts. And our immediate and instinctive reactions are not likely to suffice,
alone, against the gigantic challenge of totalitarianism.
So far we have been able to deal with that challenge at
long range — to handle it with the immense tongs of
trans-oceanic war, as if it were a radioactive danger.

But it is quite clear to me that before too long we
shall have to deal with it at first hand, within our own
society, indeed within our own minds. Instinct and impulse will not help us too much, then, for they are blind
leaders, quite as likely to serve one master as another.
American totalitarianism will not look like totalitarianism, it will look like Americanism; if we are destroyed, it will be by the divisions and uncertainties
within our own minds and society. Indeed we shall be
destroyed by our own strengths and virtues, if they
are unsupported by a framework of action and reality
far more vigorous than any we now know. Therefore
the search for that reality is urgent.

I begin by wondering whether there is not some one
form of the State, some single political theory, that is
particularly 'Christian.' But there is not much help
there. As we read history, Christianity seems to have
been almost a chameleon in its capacity to adapt to

whatever color and form the State might take, and endlessly inventive, in its best moods, to penetrate and leaven the political organism.

Lately a lot has been said and written to demonstrate that Western democracy has a peculiar dependence on Christian ideas and ideals, even to the point of claiming that it was Christianity, or perhaps even Protestant Christianity, which gave birth to democracy and its attendant conditions. I suspect that there is a measure of truth in this; and that this truth is important. But in the main it is a windy over-simplification — luncheon-club polemics — which evaporates on examination. Actually, Christianity has done very well under democracy; it has also been deep and fertile under monarchies, tyrannies, republics, totalitarian despotisms, popular revolutions, and gang warfare. And it will continue to do business, I am convinced, because of its very nature, and the stubborn facts of Divine judgment and heavenly grace.

There is a measure of truth, I repeat, in the assertion of a peculiar relation between Western political democracy and the Christian body. This I propose to return to, after a bit. But the claim of wholehearted, filial relationship one to the other is idle and mischievous.

There is not much help to be gained from the search for a uniquely Christian form of the State. Nor is there, apparently, any uniquely Christian attitude toward the State, to serve as a point of reference in our search. Certainly within historic Christianity there is extraordinary diversity; the three extreme attitudes are all centrally and respectably represented.

The attitude of withdrawal — 'I have seceded from Society' cried Tertullian during the bitter years of rivalry between the decaying Empire and the ardent and vigorous Church. 'I have chosen the camp of light, and I have no part in the camp of darkness.' That is one attitude, one relationship, running steadily from the beginning until now — the Apocalypse, Tertullian, the desert monk, the Anabaptist, Thoreau looking out of the village jail, asking plaintively, 'Waldo, what are you doing out there?', Jehovah's Witnesses — clearly it runs on in every State and every age. The Church has no relationship, no duty, to the State except that of withdrawing itself and saving itself from the ever-impending, towering ruin of earthly power.

The attitude of partnership — 'The powers that be are ordained of God' — is another attitude, running steadily from the beginning — St. Paul, St. Luke with his earnest wish to defend the Church as a *religio licita,* Ambrose, Eusebius, the Schoolmen, then certainly modern Roman theory and much Anglican thought — a sober appreciation of the ministry of earthly power under God, and a willingness to see that Church and State together were needed, in some real partnership, to complete God's plan for His children's welfare.

The attitude of identity — the totalitarian theorists, the Caesaro-papalisms, the theocracies of Geneva or New England. State and Church, Christian and citizen are but two sides to the same coin. Sometimes Caesar doubled as Pope, as in the Byzantine solution; some-times the Pope doubled as Caesar, as in Geneva; in this general theory it does not matter particularly whether head or tail turns up.

These three are the extreme attitudes; and within them the political theory and practice of Christianity has moved quite freely. As in the case of form, so in the exploration of attitude is there little positive guidance to be gotten for the inquirer who seeks to find a definitive Christian doctrine.

I stress this because I think it is important — at least it is important for me — to start thinking about our Church and our State with as few preconceptions as possible about what a Christian ought to feel or seek in his search for a just society. There is very little ortho-doxy to be guarded or worried about in either the form of the State under which Christianity thrives or the re-lation between the two.

But this very flexibility itself has been possible be-cause of certain extremely deep convictions basic to Christianity. These convictions do constitute a sort of orthodoxy on which, I am quite sure, the health of both State and Church depend. I will put what I think they are in very simple terms.

1. It is essential for the good of society that the State, whatever its form or substance, be regarded with great reserve and a profound suspicion. The classic Christian maxim would run like this: 'Remember, my children, the State is the punishment for our sins.'

2. It is essential that the State serve no absolutes, nor

pretend to fulfill absolute goals. In the darkness of this world there is none good or right 'save one, that is God.'

3. It is essential that man himself, this concrete individual, be seen always as the end and never the means, and therefore always the measure and the master of the State. 'The Sabbath was made for man.'

4. It is essential that the real power in Society be responsive to the choice and will of the people and to their needs.

5. It is essential that there be freedom in the effective areas, and most particularly freedom to associate in voluntary groups, to learn, to speak, and to pray.

Let me comment on these rubrics and then try to apply them to our own problem. First, the reserve — the suspicion — with which the State should be regarded.

The State is the organization of political power that protects the life of a society and assists in the fulfillment of that society's aims. In Lincoln's classic statement, 'the legitimate object of government is to do for the people what needs to be done, but which they cannot, by individual effort, do at all, or do so well, for themselves.' In the pursuit of that end, the major duties of the State must always be police duties, in the broadest sense — to make sure that substantial justice is done, that in the uneasy rivalry of competing activities and philosophies room is made for truth to be found, that in the darkness of imperfect knowledge men may choose as gently and wisely as they can, and that the common life is protected from harm.

One of the classic dreams of men has been the dream of a time when the State would no longer be needed. We hanker after a society of perfect men; indeed we have the myth and the hope, and myth and hope are near allied, of the good man who needs no policeman. Yet even as incorrigible a sentimentalist as Rousseau spoke for us all, exclaiming that we are born free, yet remarking soberly that we are everywhere found in chains, not chains imposed by evil power outside man but required by man's own condition. The Christian might well fail to share Rousseau's enthusiasm for the state of nature, but we should certainly agree about the origin of the chains. They, and the necessity of them, are no more than the usual and universal burden of mortality.

But the perspective is important. The State is the servant of the community, to do what is necessary to fulfill the nature and purposes of the community and to protect it against danger from without and, especially, from within. It is the servant of the community's hope and will; it is then, inevitably, the servant of the community's God.

In point of fact, the supreme contribution of Christianity to political theory is, very likely, exactly at this point. Once the classic religion had lost its authority and relevance, the classic idea of the State degenerated inevitably into a closed system. The decline and fall of the pagan Empire was very disappointing as a dramatic spectacle, as every schoolboy knows. It sounds exciting — 'The Fall of Rome' — but it was, in fact, a slow and very tedious and very undramatic death from moral starvation; the decline might be summed up by saying that the State lost its faith in anything outside of itself and ended with its tail and half its body in its mouth, trying to live on its own flesh.

We remember the valiant efforts to break out of the closed system, to keep from saying that 'the State exists in order that the State may exist.' Yet the doom was certain, once it had been conceded that the State must contain within itself its own justification, that its own peace and well-being must be its only aim. Step by step, in the deliberate choking of every breath of 'innovation,' every channel of new mission and new vitality, in the deliberate denial of any source of authority or any standard of good outside itself, the condemnation of the classic Empire was a self-condemnation.

And step by step the Empire sought for new vitality to restore its depleted tissues. Professor Cochrane sums it up in two sentences: 'Constantine had thought of Christianity as a tonic, to be administered in carefully regulated doses . . . Theodosius proposed a blood-transfusion,' believing that in Christianity 'was to be found a principle of political cohesion . . . which would ensure to the Empire a finality in keeping with her secular claims.' *

Theodosius got more than he bargained for. In Am-

* Charles Norris Cochrane, *Christianity and Classical Culture,* Oxford University Press, 1944, p. 336.

brose, for the first time, the self-enclosed, classic tradition met the perpendicular judgment of Catholic
theology. 'What you decree for others must be decreed
for you, too . . . Do not exalt yourself; if you wish to
maintain your authority, you must submit yourself to
God.' * So Ambrose, thundering against the Emperor;
so the Christian always against the State. The auton-
omous social whole conferring rights upon the individual gave way to a new conception, of the society
of individuals under God conferring rights upon the
social whole. The change was partly a Christian assertion of the individual, partly a Christian assertion of
Divine monarchy and over-ruling Providence; but
mainly it was a rejection of the self-enclosed and self-
justifying State in favor of an organic society of free
and sinful men, who give a limited power to the guardian that they may walk in peace through the darkness
to the light.

Theodosius represents the last hope of the classic
Empire. The hope failed because Christianity could
not envisage the State as a good in itself. And this rejection has remained in our blood stream ever since.
That reserve toward the State, that refusal to call the
State 'good,' save only in the most limited and derivative sense, is an essential element, I believe, in all Christian political thought.

So also is the refusal to concede to the State or to any
worldly authority the virtue of an absolute. The characteristic question of the ancient political theorist was,

* Quoted by Cochrane, op. cit., p. 348.

'What is the best government?' The characteristic Christian question has been, 'What is a free society?' Any government, any State that pretends to 'the best,' that pretends to the fulfillment of an absolute leads, inevitably, to tyranny. If the presumption to the absolute be allowed, then no man has the right to disobey. Whether it be an aristocracy or an oligarchy or a theocracy or a rule by majorities does not make much difference; the basic question is 'What are we seeking?' If it be conceded that there is a 'best' which may be known and realized by mortal men, then there is no need or value to freedom; there is only the choice of docility or treason.

Here there is no question where the central stream of Christian witness lies. What from the beginning Christianity offered the world was not an absolute, either of knowledge or of virtue, but a redeeming and sanctifying freedom under a God Who alone was good.

Our third rubric needs little comment and much application. It is the necessary complement of the first two. If the State is no more than a neutral guardian, if it is not itself, nor does it serve, an absolute, then, in the Christian scheme, a radical change in balance has occurred. Either man exists for the State, or the State for man — there is no middle ground. And against any pretension of the State to autonomy, the Christian sets the *given fact* of human society — of man and the brotherhood into which he is born, a brotherhood not created by law or kindness but by the order of the universe itself, a brotherhood of immortal souls who in themselves, wise and foolish, good and bad, are worth the cost of the Cross. It is this givenness of humanity, of the individual and society, with which the Christian begins and to which, in the end, he refers all his political thought.

The fourth and fifth principles are of a more controversial nature, I suppose. What I mean by 'real power' is simply that, in any age, political power may or may not correspond to the actual dynamics of a society. Power originates not in the State but in the society of which the State is the political expression; a free government may not mean a free society by a long shot, and it certainly will not if the actual dynamics, the 'real power,' is exercised apart from effective political control. Moreover, a free society would be itself meaningless if it were not responsive to the will of the people, either through government or in some other way.

Nazi Germany was an illustration of part of this. Under Hitler, the forms of a free government, many of them, persisted, as indeed did the fictions of a free society. Actually, the real power was exercised entirely apart from any freedom, political or social. The Imperial Japanese government was another illustration. So probably is any standard despotism anywhere. The tyrant's first principle is, 'Let them elect anybody they want, as long as I can call the turn.' The 'turn' may be financial power, land, military power, education, the

Church — whatever the substantive power is. The principle is the same. Therefore the illusion of a free government may be a very dangerous one indeed.

So too may the illusion of a free society, and for the same reason. Real freedom implies real responsibilities; real issues must be at stake, and real power awaiting the decision. To call a twentieth-century society free simply because a man can sleep late on a Sunday morning if he wants to, or can smoke what brand of cigarette he chooses, is obviously silly. Yet, as a matter of fact, an attitude toward freedom not much less trivial than that is all too often encountered in our society.

There must be freedom in the effective areas — that is the point. And in any society this means that over against the inevitable ethical monolith of the State there must be freedom for the voluntary associations of men, especially in minorities, to judge and criticize, to question, and to improvise better and conflicting solutions. The State — any State — must be by its very nature an ethical monolith. Once the practical decisions are made, whether by a king or a majority, an ethical doctrine has been established. The sound society, refusing absolutes, accepting the limitations of mortality, is prudent and careful to guard with jealous watchfulness the existence of real freedom within its own body. Its decision may be wrong; it is almost certainly imperfect; then let the voice of the free men arise to check and guide, to lead to greater light, and in their freedom make a wiser choice.

When I come to apply these maxims to our own State and society, it is hard not to feel uneasiness, if not real concern. We have seen, in our own time, the beginning of an immense change in the popular attitude toward the State. In the early days of the American experiment, it was easy for us to keep things in what I should call a Christian perspective; that is to say, to retain a healthy pessimism about the State. 'The less government the better' was our general attitude. 'It is a necessary evil and we shall put up with it, and support it, and generally try to get the wisest men we can to run it. But we shall recognize it for what it is; and we shall arrange things so, by checks and balances within and by the corrections of a free society without, that it will stay as a necessary evil and a penalty for our sins.'

The change I refer to does not lie in the fact that there is more government than there used to be, or that government takes more money in taxes or has more power. Those are the popular points of attack, and they are largely secondary and specious ones. Any realistic person, seeing the changes in our way of life from a small and sparse rural economy to a massive and complex technical one knows that the State must follow those changes and accommodate to them. To give effective control to a vastly more complicated society, the State requires greater power, which means more money and more bureaucrats.

The bureaucratifying of the State worries us too much — it is the beatifying of the State that is the danger signal. The change and the danger lie in the assumption, largely unconscious, largely unspoken, that the State is good. A free society can safely afford almost any assumption of government power in an emergency, or undergo the most drastic adaptation, as long as we understand what we are doing, who is the master, and where the source of goodness lies. But confusion in principles is fatal.

Of course I should agree that government at all levels hires too many people and spends too much money and has too much power. Governments always do; and they always need to be checked. It is an essential as well as a pleasant duty of free citizens to 'kick the rascals out.' But the exercise of this freedom will not solve the basic problem. A beneficent State under Republican auspices will be no more tolerable than a Democratic one. A State pretending to be good and to do good is as odious under one label as another. A free society and a Christian society requires more than political freedom; they require a godly skepticism toward any worldly pretension to goodness at all.

However, and this is a point for preachers, the reason why the State is moving more and more into the role of the benevolent parent is that the free and voluntary agencies of kindness and wisdom have not kept pace with the actual needs of people. If you want to understand the massive phenomenon of the twentieth-century Welfare State, this preposterous Beadle, you have only to read and meet again the 'porochial beadle' of nineteenth-century *Oliver Twist*. Mr. Bumble represented the breakdown of an antiquated, cold, sub-Christian, post-Christian charity; Mr. Bumble died and was buried; and in his place came the gigantic Beadle of the Welfare State — a dreadful figure dispensing charity, 'carefully iced,' not in the name now of a 'cautious, statistical Christ,' but in the name of a faceless anonymity, the State, born not of pity or charity but of human selfishness and pride and of the substitute for the optional God.

Any State is a Welfare State — that is the State's reason for being. The phrase is meaningless except as it signifies the new superstition of people to whom personal responsibility and personal relationships have become dim and unreal. This superstition, that a necessary evil can both be good in itself and confer good, is the most dangerous of all political illusions. But it is inevitable in a society in which men and women in their voluntary associations do not accept the given facts of human brotherhood and human need. To use a familiar image, in this as in other matters, where there is a vacuum in society the State rushes in, and must, by its very nature, fill it.

I know that history does not repeat itself. Yet I cannot hear the ancient cry *panem et circenses,* or remember an ancient emptiness of heart, and not think long about our own contemporaries who know no God except a legislature and acknowledge no debt save those established by law. For myself, I do not choose to be loved or pitied by a legislature.

A second comment on American political life, put

simply, is this. Our basic philosophy, as I understand it, is that the majority has the right to decide. We have carefully avoided saying that the majority is right. Generally speaking, I think they have commonly been wrong, as things turned out; certainly the majority has a bad enough record to make anybody suspicious. Over and over again in our history it has been Lincoln who has read his Bible aright, and the two-score wise men who have been proved wrong in the event.

But, in our system, it does not matter. We have never pretended that the majority was right. We have simply agreed that in this mortal passage the majority shall have the right to decide the practical steps by which we shall all be guided. It is, of course, a basically theological reservation. The Christian skepticism about absolutes, widened and implemented by sixteen centuries of political experience, is one of the major contributions of Christianity to our American political tradition. You may read the Federalist Papers almost at random — there will scarcely be a page that does not reflect this skepticism or foresee the need for ample defense against the absolutist assumptions.

On the positive side, our correctives are found in many areas. Most tangibly, they are found in the political structure itself, in the sometimes cumbersome system of checks and balances, in the compromise settlements, like that of having both a Senate and a House of Representatives, and, supremely, in the guarantees of civil liberties.

Less tangible, the correctives appear in our determination that all political decisions be open ones, openly arrived at. Perhaps the most significant guarantee here is that of judicial review. The Supreme Court cannot make a majority right; it does not usually pretend to; but it guarantees that the processes of a free society will have every opportunity to function, in the light.

But the best guarantees in the world will not function well in an apathetic society. The majority will always tend to arrogate omniscience to itself; the majority will always be tempted to ignore unimportant opposition and crush the important one; and the only ultimate safeguard is in the resolution of free men not only to guard the minorities and guard the eccentric and guard the exceptional, but to foster as well among themselves, in free association with one another, the search for wiser choices and clearer truth.

Here we see as well as anywhere the principle of effective and responsible power and freedom. Nobody minds the crank who protests loudly against the decimal system or the use of paper money. A majority state gladly tolerates the harmless eccentric who objects in an area where his objection cannot possibly mean anything. The toleration of the important minorities, the freedom of the eccentrics who matter, is a different story. It is there, in times of stress, that the vigilance of determined men, and most particularly the vigilance of the Church, is most required.

There is no earthly power that can keep a State or a majority from absolutizing itself, if the people themselves give up the fight. A democratic State will deify itself just as fast as Imperial Rome did, if the people do not believe in a Kingdom not of this world. An optional god is no god; if he holds no effective sway over the wills of men, then the god of this world, the god of the State, will take the power and reign. He will take it, not because he has defeated free men but because they have not fought for their birthright.

Then there is this final comment about American life: the question of *real power* is a severe and urgent one today. In any society, one of the basic tests is whether or not the real power is responsive to adequate controls. Two questions are involved always. One is the definition of real power. The other is the choice of control.

By and large, in our society, the real power is principally collected in technical and industrial processes. The wealth of the nation and the livelihood of the largest group of its citizens center in our industry. Our other powers in large part are founded upon industrial power.

The characteristic form in which that power is organized is the corporation. The corporation is a peculiar modern development, growing out of a certain fiction about ownership, because, at the time of its birth, ownership was the characteristic form of the control and use of wealth.

In this fiction, the industrial plant is owned by many owners, who elect managers to operate it and employ workers to produce the goods. In the same fiction, responsible control is exercised within the ancient moral fabric of ownership.

In point of fact, as we have known for a generation, this fiction is almost totally meaningless and useless as an adequate control. In fact, the stockholder exercises almost no control over the company he owns. He has abdicated control willingly, to a management which of necessity becomes self-perpetuating. In fact the ordinary stockholder does not want ownership and its attendant responsibilities. He really wishes simply to rent his money. He commonly will have almost no idea how his company operates, or what its labor policies are, or perhaps even what it produces.

It would be quite unfair to blame management for this abdication. A good many commentators have pointed out that actually management has fought against it more than a little. American management, by and large, is as conscientious and responsible a group of men as could be found; they are not a rapacious class of exploiters, jealous for power; they are intelligent and sensitive men who, whether they wanted to or not, have had to cope with the fact of irresponsible ownership. The problem is not a supposed ruthlessness on their part — the problem is the real vacuum of responsibility. Management cannot accept a responsibility that belongs to the owner. They cannot even accept responsibility to the owner as their employer. The owner does not wish it, nor could he now accept it if he did wish it.

Therefore we have arrived at a critical juncture in

American life. The effective power, by and large, is ownerless and irresponsible, rolling around in the hold of the ship like a cargo broken loose. Management joins forces to master and use it; labor bands together to counterbalance management; but at the heart there is still irresponsibility. And the State does what the State irresistibly must — it controls, more and more. For if Society will not make up its mind how to exact responsible use of its resources, then the State, *faute mieux*, will seize them. The State, like the great dumb ox that it is, shoves into any empty stall.

It is all well enough for industrial men to rail at controls. If they do not devise a better system, then they must be content with political management. Many businessmen are aware of the anomalous situation in which they live; they do not like it; they do not like the degree of social power the modern corporation exercises; they do not like the obligations entailed by the control they actually wield. But for all the technical and commercial ingenuity of our people, we have shown almost no social inventiveness in this area, save, perhaps, to diffuse ownership as widely as possible.

Indeed, from the Christian body there has been little more inventiveness. Paralyzed by the inherited fiction of ownership, by the dogma of the optional God, by the professionalizing of the Church, we were aware of the problem, at least of its symptoms; but I cannot now recall any major discussion of it as a problem in moral theology, nor have I heard very many Christian laymen explore the possible solutions to it. Only within the last two or three years has the National Council of Churches begun a rather gingerly study of a problem that, at least since the publication of Berle and Means's massive book * a generation ago, should have been in the forefront of our attention.

For it all comes back to very simple quantities in the end. We spend half an hour or half a lifetime try-ing to cope with these great abstractions — Society, the State, Power; and we grow more and more dis-mayed by the apparent monstrous size and complexity of them. But sooner or later we are led to see that the actual form of human society itself is extraordinarily simple and clear.

This very morning, at the altars in their parish churches, millions of people saw and re-enacted the fundamental pattern of human society — *a commu-nity in communion.* There is no further political wis-dom to be learned than what Christians rehearse, day after day, at the Lord's Table, if they will only learn it. If we can put behind us the professionalized, secu-larized trappings of our liturgies, if we can stop trying to understand them as 'religious' acts and can see them as expressing the underlying reality of Society, we shall have made the essential beginning of our mission to this post-Christian world.

For a community is far more than the world suspects, and requires far more, and gives far more. A commu-nity is not a place; it is not people alone. In every gener-

* Adolf Berle, Jr., and Gardiner C. Means, *The Modern Corporation and Private Property,* New York, Macmillan, 1933.

ation men think they can clear a little space, push back the desert, and establish a civilized community. But

'The desert is not remote in southern tropics . . .
The desert is squeezed in the tube-train next to you,
The desert is in the heart of your brother.' *

Indeed, the desert is in our hearts, most of all. Therefore civilization is never more than one generation deep; it is no stronger or more durable than one man's choice; it is never safe. Therefore a community is more than a place and more than the people. It is a network of obligations shared, a web of responsibilities and freedoms accepted and sustained by the will of free men.

A community requires place and people; but it has imperative need also for freedom within itself, for the privilege of offering itself, and for judgment over and beyond its own ends and needs.

Freedom, offering, judgment — these are the absolute necessities of a true community. If the Lord's Supper were no more than a parable, we should still have seen these things represented. We should have seen a natural community, gathered together in a voluntary association, making a corporate and voluntary offering before the symbol of a judging truth that unites all of the separate selves. This any man can see in the great Christian liturgy, even if only as a natural parable.

And it is a knowledge that has leavened Western

* T. S. Eliot, *The Rock,* New York, Harcourt, Brace and Company, 1934, p. 9.

society. Like 'hocus-pocus,' a phrase that carries us back to another and greater mystery dimly remembered, so does the word 'community' still bear some of the ancient color of the word 'communion,' without our consciously realizing the source of the overtones.

But the Eucharist is not only a parable of what we wish Society were like; it is the reality itself. There is no further truth than this immortal transaction. I say again, it is not a 'religious' or 'cultic' truth. This is the way men really are. This is the given pattern of human society.

The community of the communion is a place and people, but it is supremely the locus of freedom and offering and judgment, those indispensable characteristics of any full and healthy society.

Here there is the free recognition of the givenness of man. Here men come not for fear or favor but simply because they are men. Nobody is 'good enough' to come, or strong enough to take what has already freely been given him. Men find a unity already established, not contrived by law or custom or advantage, but given. Watch separate people come into a church some time, and see them kneel, one by one, and see how wonderfully the common posture suddenly shows how deep the unity has been all along. Penitence, hope, charity — these are not simply the keynotes of our individual preparation for holy communion. They are the basic social virtues expressed without words, long before we can put words to them.

Here there is the uniting of all the separate selves, in

awareness of one another, in charity, and supremely in the act of offering. What will you do with your separateness? What will you do with your life and your work? What else can you do, if it is worth anything at all, save offer it to that One alone Who is good enough to receive it, and Who will use it to nourish and sustain the brotherhood?

Here there is the liberating and uniting fact of judgment. The altar is a throne as well as a table. The offering itself is the beginning of the judgment; the shadow of the Cross lies upon it; the hands that receive and lift it to the Eternal Father are wounded hands; the redeemed community fed by it is the community of the Word.

These are not 'religious' truths or optional truths. The first mission of the Church is to look at what lies at the heart of her community. If she does that, and sees the act as well as the parable, and if she does not linger too long in post-communion devotions, she will bring to our society precisely the saving skepticism and the saving hope we require.

To put it into its coldest terms, it is the mission of the Church to be the principal free association within the body of society. In the ancient phrase, she is 'the world's soul'; she is the organ whereby personal responsibility and the vivid individuality of men is continually reborn. She is the type community from which other communities should draw their strength. She is the vessel of judgment, of the perpendicular Word which keeps a narcissistic society from idolizing itself. She is the truly radical body in society, eternally skeptical of the faceless absolutes, eternally vigilant for the free minorities, eternally inventive to improvise new social and political solutions to timeless needs. She is the medicine against a State that tries to be its own justification because she asks always the question 'To whom are you offering what you do, and who will value it and use it?' She is the household where men are accepted as what they are, and where they meet one another in dignity and gentleness, and in a common hope which carries them all together.

It is her Mission to be those things.

III

LOWER THAN THE ANGELS

EVERY FREE society, for the sake of its own existence, must provide three things for its children:

It must transmit to them its accumulated store of knowledge — facts, and the techniques for acquiring and evaluating facts.

It must prepare them to take their proper place as members of the society.

It must teach them the standards of judgment on which the life of the society depends and how to be guided by them; it must teach them how to choose and how to take sides.

These are not separate and distinct processes, actually; they happen best when they happen together. Taken altogether, they comprise the educational process of a society. The schools and colleges of a society exist for these purposes.

Sniping at the public schools is a favorite indoor sport in America. In the public-dinner-Women's-Auxiliary-Chamber-of-Commerce circuit where I spend a great deal of my time, no function would be complete without a suitable report of the latest horrors of public education. Well, it is a free country — but I am moved sometimes to feel that much of the criticism, even that originating in the Church, is pointless and useless.

In part, the public schools and colleges are what people want them to be. If public education is getting to be more and more of a colossal baby-sitting operation, which keeps children out of the way until they can go to work, I cannot feel that it is anybody's fault but our own. We have shoved onto the shoulders of the school more and more of what in an earlier day centered around home and church; and we have done it because it was easier to do it that way. Any priest trying to arrange a confirmation class or choir rehearsal knows how hard it is to find a waking hour when the children are not engaged in some extra-curricular activity. It makes his life difficult. He should not stop there, however, but should go on to examine the desiccation of the other centers of social life for children, most of all their own homes and the parish houses of their churches.

In a deeper sense, too, schools are what we want them to be. The flabbiness of teaching itself, the steady lessening of actual intellectual accomplishment, the steady easing of academic standards and requirements — all this has happened because, on the whole, it was more trouble than people cared to take to think hard about what their children should learn and to insist that they learn it. Colleges blame lower standards on high schools for not preparing youngsters better. High schools blame them on colleges for not requiring more. A pox on both houses; the main problem is that the people themselves have not known what they really wanted nor insisted that they get it.

A second class of criticism arises from the fact that sometimes we ask the impossible. A lot of the attack from religious sources has been of this type. We have really been saying that the school should do, religiously, what no school could possibly do — make good Christians out of children. God alone will do that; and next to Him, parents will; and next to them, the contagion of Christian fellowship. But parents have sent their offspring to school in the same mood in which they send them to Sunday School, partly to get them out of the way, partly to have them taught in some mysterious way a kind of life to which the parents themselves only partially subscribe. This kind of sabotage alone makes the average Sunday School a hopeless problem at the outset; and a day school can hardly be blamed for making little headway against a parental abdication that violates most of the child's natural loyalties and relationships at the beginning.

Then too, much of the criticism really arises out of a growing discomfiture at what the whole secular experiment means, when we see it spelled out in terms of public education. It has only been a hundred years since Horace Mann wrestled with the problem of religious instruction in public schools in Massachusetts. He sought to find a common body of agreed Christian teaching that could be incorporated in a public system.

He could not find it. The divisions of Christians alone prevented his finding it.

This year, under Congregational rule, the Rev. Mr. So and So, and the Rev. Doctor So and So will be on the Committee; but next year, these Reverends and Reverend Doctors will be plain Misters, — never having had apostolic consecration from the Bishop. This year, the ordinance of baptism is inefficacious without immersion; next year one drop of water will be as good as forty fathoms.*

And reluctantly, and with a pessimistic judgment on education without religious teaching at the heart of it, he abandoned his hopes.

In that hundred years we have moved, in practice and in theory, to the present fantastic situation, which amounts in fact but not in intention, I am sure, to the establishment of the Religion of the Optional God as the State religion. It is a situation profoundly disturbing to the teacher as well as to the churchman. The thoughtful teacher knows quite as well as we do the futility of trying to communicate an understanding of a Christian civilization without ever being able to teach the reality on which it is founded; this task is like trying to teach human biology on the assumption that storks bring babies, and that science takes over from there.

Secularism poses a teaching problem as acute in its way as the religious problem it also poses. And much of

* Raymond B. Culver, *Horace Mann and Religion in the Massachusetts Public Schools*, New Haven, Yale University Press, 1929, p. 208.

the distaste for the present unhappy and uneasy armis-
tice may actually be a creative movement. I pray that
it may be; I can see nothing but disaster ahead if the
present crippling and imprisoning secularism of public
schools continues. In the meantime, however, there is
little point in carping at a State agency for not doing
something they are forbidden by public law to do, and
in large part could not do anyway.

Well, all this is simply a plea for fair-mindedness. In
our criticism I suggest that we start with the frank
recognition that the American system of State education is the solution we came to, and would still come
to, considering the real problems of a pluralistic society
like our own. What distinguishes the American system
is not that it is a system of 'free, public education';
there have been other systems of free, public education, largely under religious auspices. The principal
characteristic of the American system is the fact that
it is a *State* system, a public system administered not by
a voluntary agency within society but by the political
organization of society itself. This is an important dis-
tinction.

But it is a *fact:* and it is the choice of a free society.

It has brought many good things into American life.
If I do not try to list them, it is not because I am not
aware of them. Opportunities, equipment, the cross-
breeding of diverse strains, racial and religious, the re-
duction of illiteracy — the good things are many and
real, and we should not have got them any other way.
To recall Lincoln's phrase, 'the legitimate object of

government is to do for the people what needs to be done, but which they cannot . . . do for themselves.' This is the charter of State education, along with the myriad other functions we have delegated to the State in the ever-changing frontier of political and social decision.

This frontier of decision is a fluid one. It changes from day to day, never without searching of heart, never without unexpected consequence. Some decisions are more basic than others. A private army is a lot more distasteful to American eyes than a private school, so much so that we should not permit it without a major constitutional convulsion. The Railway Express Agency may carry parcels for us, but it had better not print money. But fashions change, and needs alter, and what is 'Socialism' to one generation is open and public necessity to another.

All I am saying is that a practical decision, like that of State education, needs to be appraised and examined like anything else the State does. To call State education a good in itself is about the most fatuous comment I can imagine. It is like saying that only hydrant water can put out a fire. The native Christian reserve toward the State applies to education as well as to anything else. You may accept the decision gladly, because it may be the only possible one for the moment. But to absolutize it is immensely dangerous, and nowhere more so than in as delicate and vital a process as the educational one. No one is going to argue very much about whether it is better to be arrested by a policeman or by a Pinkerton detective; there may be slightly more prestige in the latter, but the penalty for lifting a mink coat is the same under either system. We do not take any such flippant attitude toward a school, however, for it concerns the very soul of society itself.

Therefore our need of reserve, of steadfast refusal to absolutize, is an imperative one. It is always quite possible that a better solution can be found. It is always urgent that we continually examine our successive decisions, and that we keep open every channel of free exploration and comparison in society itself.

The independent school — the free school as contrasted with the State school — plays its most important part in this connection. The independent school is far from being an ideal balance to the State school; it has neither the resources nor the problems of the State school; but we have no better check than this, nor can we hope to have a better one at present.

To say 'a better solution' means, first of all, that we examine our present solution against the problem it is supposed to solve. The problem is how this society of ours is to get its threefold task accomplished: the transmission of knowledge, the training in citizenship, and the teaching of judgment so that our children may choose more wisely than we have and be able to take one more step toward the light.

Our own educational philosophy wrestles principally with the second purpose. Certainly the idea of communicating information is under something of a cloud in popular circles; and much of the third purpose is simply impossible to achieve in the secular solution, as it is now accepted. An optional God would not judge human society with any great force. If you cannot learn about God and His will at the same time and in the same way as you learn about history and politics, you will never understand history very well, or politics or God either, and you will never be able to take sides for the good of society, which is the prime duty of a citizen.

Necessarily the second purpose looms largest in the secular school. And it is this emphasis that the State school serves best, in many areas. The composite society, of diverse beliefs and backgrounds, into which a child is plunged; and the experience he has of rubbing elbows with everybody else; and the wisdom he can learn about how to get along positively and usefully with his fellow citizens; and the sense he gains of the reality of society over and above the accidental variations within it — these are important opportunities of immense consequence to society. And the degree of curiosity and inventiveness lavished on this phase of education in our time is simply enormous.

We still have segregation, with its impoverishment of society — racial segregation, neighborhood segregation. We have human and therefore imperfect teachers who import prejudice. There is too much tinkering in this area and too little recognition that solid knowledge, facts, and information, have a lot more to do with attitudes than playing antiseptic little games in the classroom. In point of fact we are altogether too self-conscious about these purposes as being separate, and we do not see clearly enough that actually all three purposes are at work together in a good school, all the time, and cannot be dealt with separately. A classroom exercise in racial tolerance is likely to remain just that until a child is helped in his instincts by a little solid information about American history, and a few facts about biology, and until he has learned something about God and the Samaritans.

But with all these negative comments, the fact remains that the State school has done an incalculably useful job in this area, and a better one, by and large, than any voluntary school could have done.

Currently I imagine the greatest amount of dissatisfaction is with the handling of the first purpose, the transmission of knowledge. Three forces are at work here to cause that dissatisfaction.

One is the tendency inherent in any democratic process, to level down rather than up — the ineradicable tendency to mediocrity, and to the sometimes deliberate adoption of mediocrity as an end. Public schools are far too impressed with their problem of having to teach every child, bright or dull. There is no novelty in that. Preachers have been doing that since the beginning of time. And rulers have had to make laws, and judges have had to apply them to exactly the same cross section.

It is only when a school system loses sight of its broader purposes, and concentrates exclusively on the single phase of being a stage through which young men

and women pass, that the cross section becomes a problem. If the primary object of a school were to keep children off the streets until they are sixteen, then the questions of truth and knowledge would be irrelevant. But
if the transmission of truth be as central as I suppose it
is, then the educational process is a very different story.

For truth is the most aristocratic master we know.
None can attain to it fully; to those few to whom great
knowledge is open, it comes only after arduous and
passionate search. It is no kindness to a child to let him
suppose that twelve years or sixteen years of contiguity
to books will make him a master of truth. He knows
better than that, by instinct alone, and then he discovers that, apparently, society sets no such store by
the prize. That discouraging discovery is what too
many children make as they go through their school
years. The people who surround them, who pay the
taxes and make the money, do not seem to hold excellence in such high esteem. The child grows accustomed
to an industry which, for its own prosperity, must dis-
dain excellence; indeed he will probably earn his living not by excellence but by deliberate mediocrity.
He has heard the common man praised as the lord and
master, and he will not learn, perhaps until he is old,
that the uncommon man is the only one who matters.
He has grown too familiar with averages and abstractions and has come to feel the most deadly coldness in
his own heart, the fear that perhaps he is only a fraction and a means himself in some impersonal system of
blind and indiscriminating power.

This is the method of mediocrity; the genesis of it lies deep in the heart of an insecure people unsustained by a vigorous and certain faith in God. Mediocrity is basically a theological problem, which rises in acute form in any free society. There is no easy answer to it. But the chief bulwark against it is in two places — Church and school.

The more a school system fosters a feeling that the only things that matter are the things everybody can learn, the more it fosters a vague egalitarianism which stunts and discourages the exceptional child and deprives all children of whole ranges of knowledge simply because they are 'hard' and unsuited to the average, to that degree the school fails in one of its essential purposes. It is no shame to fail an examination, if examinations are necessary. It is no unkindness for a child to discover that there are some things he cannot do well, and others he can. He will discover that soon enough, unless he is deliberately deluded. Indeed he has already discovered it and the principle of excellence too, from the first time he has ever tried to understand his father's words or tried to build a tower out of his blocks. He needs desperately more faith in excellence and in the aristocracy of all good things, for his very soul itself will depend sometime on a truth, like freedom or beauty or love or the straightness of a line, that will be forever beyond him, yet is the unchanging and saving guide for his life.

But our schools do fail there, too often. 'The pursuit of excellence' — Plato's far-away phrase — has little relevance in the contemporary school. And without that drive toward the unattainable, standards are emptied of force and fail in their purpose.

An equally dangerous tendency is the attitude that only certain kinds of knowledge are important. The 'Liberal Arts' major at a state university not infrequently feels he is something of a curiosity. All too often he feels he must fall into one of three categories; either (a) he is studying for the ministry, (b) he is the child of a teacher of English, or (c) he has not made up his mind what he is going to be when he grows up. And even these exceptions are being weeded out, it seems — unless he is lucky, the poor divinity student is likely to be shoved off into that bootless monstrosity known as a 'pre-theological course'; and the chances of a boy surviving into college years without having been vocationally tested, classified, and predetermined grow daily smaller and smaller. Soon, we may fear, the only students doing the liberal arts will be the wretched children of the people who teach those arts. Such is the nightmare caricature suggested by many a university catalogue, and by the analysis of many a graduating class.

Actually, of course, the picture is quite different on many campuses. The most significant movement in independent colleges in the last generation has been the counter-current to this, in the re-establishment of a general education for all except the most extraordinary case. Even in the state colleges, whose autonomy is far more restricted, a parallel movement has taken place. All this is good. If the college did not have to spend so much time teaching what the high school should have taught, the situation would be a lot better. The ordinary American high school in this year of Grace is, as an educational experience, the most elaborate waste of time a free society has yet devised. And it drags the whole enterprise down with it.

A free society must have access to all truth. If a people is to be its own master, then society must take the greatest care, as Disraeli said, that its master be educated. This means the unpopular and the unutilitarian studies as well as the fashionable ones. The knowledge of the ancient world and the impact of Christianity upon it, the knowledge of the histories of other peoples and their civilization, the knowledge of the painstaking techniques by which the natural world is known and mastered (human nature included), the knowledge of languages and ideas, the knowledge of past prayers and vanished hopes — all this is needed in a free society. And every school must be measured ceaselessly against this standard.

A true course of studies cannot be found simply by an appeal to absolutes. There is no 'right' curriculum. Any curriculum is a matter of degree to which no universal, substantive answer can be made, least of all in the vacuum of a lecture or a book. The only answer is a relative one, determined in every generation by what is possible. The way a curriculum is determined is by conflict between impossibles. It can never be determined solely by what seems germane and desirable to a given society; for the very essence of teaching may well be to introduce into that society a perspective it lacks or a skill it has forgotten. I sometimes think that the only possible curriculum is to start with all truth and to teach as fast and as much as you can until your students finally escape! Certainly the opposite method, of teaching only what seems immediately useful to the man your student probably will be in the society you guess he will inhabit, is blindness and tyranny of the worst sort. The attempt to teach all truth is not just an Olympian impracticality. The most impractical man is the man who is nourished on the delusion of omniscience, who knows only a few skills which are soon irrelevant and outmoded. The practical man is the man who may know no skills to begin with, save how to read and think, but who understands how to learn them, and which ones he wants, and why he wants them. He stands erect in a changing world, that man, and he gives vitality to his society.

The third problem is that of the teachers themselves and their training. They reflect the strength and the weaknesses of the whole process; and it is no secret that, like the ministry and some of the other great professions, teaching does not readily attract the kind of men and women who ought to teach. Why?

It is partly a matter of the conventional pattern of a useful life. Parsons and teachers are not 'productive' in the usual sense; they are like poets and soldiers and others of that ilk; and to a world dominated by 'productivity' they live a sorry alternative to a useful life.

It is partly because teaching is about as hard a job as any life offers. No doubt there are many reasons. The facts are that preaching and teaching are two of the less attractive professions to the majority of able and qualified men and women. In the case of teachers, I sometimes think that perhaps the chief reason is the extraordinary amount of specializing and professionalizing that has gone on in recent years. There are all the courses in method, all the specialized summer schools in techniques, all the masters' degrees in theory ground out year by year — until it is no wonder that many a poor teacher is little better educated than her pupils, save only in the jargon of a specialized training! Surely there are worthy people who can be found to do various supervisory chores and to help teachers out with special problems, and run the school systems. But what a waste of potentially good teachers, to make them spend so much time in technical details that it leaves little time or energy for the heart of what they are going to teach! This is what makes teaching so unattractive to so many young men and women. They would like to teach, but they have no desire to become 'educators' and get involved in the confused technicalities of this or that educational philosophy.

College teachers are a good deal better off in that respect, except perhaps in the social sciences, where I understand they are now becoming 'educators.' But at all levels there has been a general and observable lowering of morale and of the classic self-respect of teachers. If a person is an able teacher, he is soon snapped up into some administrative chore; if he is not particularly able, he is still crammed with techniques and rarely encouraged to learn more or read more in his own field. I do not expect a young girl fresh out of college to be a monument of learning; I expect her to know what an intelligent girl should and to be able to guide my children to find truth and learn how to find it. I certainly do not want a tentative psychologizer tinkering with my children's habits, or telling me what is the matter with my family, or with American society in general. But all our training, especially at the postgraduate level, seems directed to the latter end.

Well, disregard the personal comments; the facts are that for a variety of reasons (and I say again that many of the same things are true about the ministry) teaching as a career has not drawn its share of the keenest and best minds in our time. I have seen too many of my own best students turn away from it, for these reasons, to have any doubt about it. And the teaching process, the communication of truth, has suffered accordingly.

These are some of the reasons for the vast amount of dissatisfaction with State schools, particularly in respect to their efficiency in the transmission of knowledge.

My own deepest questions lie in still another area. Let me say again that society proposes to do three things in her educational process — to transmit her knowledge, to train her children for mature participation, and to teach them the standards and secrets of the free self-criticism and judgment that is the soul of a society. Our State schools do a fair job in the first area and a better one in the second. The third area is appallingly difficult, and our record is not good. Yet it is really the most important of the three, as far as the well-being of our society is concerned.

The core of our inherited free society is a distinctively Christian attitude toward the State — a steady refusal to admit the State as a good in itself or to accept the State's welfare as an absolute.

Man is not that good or wise; he is made lower than the angels; he is free and responsible, yet he is also sinful and in darkness; therefore every act of man is under judgment. 'There is none good or right save one, that is God.'

We might go far in accepting the practical decisions of the State, but in the end there is One who judgeth and ruleth. And the covenant of love and justice between God and His children is the basic loyalty of all.

That vertical component led Western society into strange and difficult passages sometimes, into the abuses of a clerical state as truly as to heroic protests and courage. But it left a mark indelible even in these post-Christian days, in the new understanding that a true community is, first of all, built around a standard of judgment. Furthermore, if it be a true community, there is freedom within it for the constant play of that corrective judgment.

How careful we have been, even when we could not tell why, to guard the inner freedom and the eternal justice that were the medicine of the body politic. Nowhere is that care more needed than in that most critical area, the area where our children learn how to judge and what to judge by.

It is here, of course, that the limitations of the optional God press most strongly. How shall we keep, in American life, the ancient dimensions of man without the vision of God? How shall we go on supporting the audacious speculation of freedom, without the one Free Person continually before our eyes? Our faith in reason — what is it without the Word? Our gentleness and delicacy toward the dissenter, the minority, the exceptional — how shall we maintain it without the certainty of the Father who has made us all of one blood? How shall we teach what faith has given us if we may not teach the Faith? When thoughtless people say that the Church wants simply to capture the State schools for her own aggrandizement, do they never ask these questions of themselves? A man can live on his father's money or his grandfather's. But the old adage runs that 'It is three generations from shirt sleeves to shirt sleeves'; and there is no reason to suppose that a moral inheritance lasts any longer than a financial one.

Somehow society needs to cleanse the spring of judgment and faith again that the waters may run clear. Otherwise, the meanings of words, half forgotten, and the very reasons for our political institutions themselves, and the means of purifying them, will be lost. Indeed, clouds larger than a man's hand are there to be seen — a growing servility to the State, a growing cult of brutality, a carelessness about personal responsibilities and personal loyalties, a coarsening and slackening of public service, a deadening in letters and speech to the classic outlines of this enigmatic man, the eternal barbarism which reappears in every generation. We need to learn how to understand ourselves and our nature and destiny, and how to take sides with humility and resolution. This is in the end the greatest duty of the school.

I think there would not be many who would disagree with us, to this point. In or out of school circles, concern grows about what is variously called 'character training,' the 'teaching of values,' the 'spiritual foundations of our society,' or other such phrases. To take the top of the list, I cite a paragraph from a booklet of a year ago, *Moral and Spiritual Values in the Public Schools,* issued by a committee of the National Education Association. It begins:

A great and continuing purpose of education has been the development of moral and spiritual values . . . those values which, when applied in human behaviour, exalt and refine life and bring it into accord with the standards of conduct that are approved in our democratic culture . . . No society can survive without a moral order . . . no social invention however ingenious, no improvements in government structure however prudent, no enactment of statutes and ordinances however lofty their aims, can produce a good and secure society if personal integrity, honesty, and self discipline are lacking.*

I should make three reservations about this statement, direct and simple and strong as it is. One is that it is exceedingly dangerous, I think, to define moral and spiritual values as those that produce conformity to 'the standards of conduct which are approved in our democratic culture.'

I would be uncomfortable with that phrase, because I do not know what it means. What is an approved standard in our democratic culture? Who approves? By what right? Does might or a majority decide? If all that our public education does is bring about conformity with the majority's decision, then it is a poor thing and idolatrous, and the sooner it is gone the better.

I know, however, that is not what is meant. What such a sentence indicates is precisely the attempt to capitalize an inherited income — to freeze social mores at a point and say 'This is what is good and we shall preserve and teach it. We have inherited brotherhood, democracy, and equality; they are desirable; and we shall try to perpetuate them.' But there is no way under the skies to quick-freeze a way of life. It is vital and dynamic; it grows out of actual beliefs; it may be picked and eaten, but it will not keep long.

Nor are we helped, and this is my second reservation,

* *Moral and Spiritual Values in the Public Schools,* Educational Policies Commission, National Education Association, Washington, D.C., 1951, pp. 3 and 4.

by speaking of a way of life in terms of a sense of 'values.' The people who wrote this booklet are skillful teachers; they know that until a value is actualized and seen as a consequence of a factual situation somewhere, it has no real life or relevance at all. Later on they illustrate this by citing an example of a boy who inadvertently received an unmerited ten cents extra in change, and how various teachers utilized this experience to inculcate moral values. This is true to life; and every teacher appeals to some set of sanctions, some structure of reality, to support her moral teaching. Of course she does: there is no 'value' apart from the scheme of reality that validates it. Man's only choice is 'what reality do I choose?' Some will pick the authority of the State, some the pressure of shame, some the liking of comrades, some the pain of a teacher's disapproval — all derivative, all in turn depending on the one basic question, 'what is the universe really like?'

The 'is' comes before the 'ought' — this is a theological adage as old as the hills. It is well to remember it when we discuss values.

A value is a poor thing, all by itself. It is a dried prune, ethically speaking, which carries us over the winter until the tree bears again. Yet what else can a State school do, under the present settlement, except try to teach desiccated 'values'? I do not know. That is why I am fearful of what the end of this experiment will be.

My third reservation is that I think it is hopeless to

wave away history as if it had no importance. There is no absolute or universal set of values. They come to us in a matrix — encased in a particular series of events and beliefs. They are quite arbitrary, because life is arbitrary. This is not a neutral society, it is a post-Christian one. And the job of teaching values as if you could extract them from the thin air or blow them like soap bubbles out of your unconscious is simply impossible. The optional God poses an appalling teaching problem, to which there is no satisfactory solution.

Finally let me give you two words that describe the Church's mission in education. They are 'penetration' and 'partnership.'

To say that the Church accepts the secular school sounds like Margaret Fuller saying 'I accept the universe!' And we remember Carlisle's growl, 'By gad, she'd better!' Of course we accept it; it is the best we can do and it has given us immeasurable value. In this divided society there is no other solution possible, for the moment. But the Church must always stand over against the school, oblique to it; and she must be in two moods at the same time.

One mood is what I call 'penetration.' At every point and in every way it is the Church's duty to society to leaven the lump. That means a multitude of duties.

It means the reinforcement of teaching as a Christian ministry, for the laity and especially for the clergy. I say 'especially for the clergy,' because the real dimension of our penetration will mean not only bearing witness in teaching but will mean the actual creation of the Christian community within the school and particularly the college. I am not scornful of the laity. I do not know where we could find greater loyalty or a more devoted witness than in a teacher's life. I only say what the laity already know, that their witness is incomplete until it is buttressed by the whole Christian body. The courageous Christian laymen on the faculty of a state university needs and is entitled to more than what a chaplaincy on the periphery can do; he needs to speak and live as part of a whole community; and that requires the whole ministry — it requires men whose pastorate will be teaching.

Penetration requires the writing of books, and the planned and coherent invasion of graduate studies. It is simply incredible to reflect on what has happened in what are called the social sciences in American university life. Anthropology, sociology, psychology — even philosophy itself — are fields that have, for all practical purposes in one university after another, been abandoned to one single point of view, and a secularist one. There is no excuse for it except that Christian people have been so busy selling soap and preaching sermons and drilling for oil — or if they were teachers they were running Church boarding schools — that they could not be bothered.

Other fields have suffered from that same abdication in lesser degree. It is an astonishing thing that for all the millions of dollars expended every year in 'missionary strategies' for the conversion of America, there has never been a concerted strategy for the most important missionary area of them all, the writing of books and the training of teachers.

Penetration — penetration by Christian parents in P.T.A.'s, penetration by pastors on school boards, penetration by Christian writers who will write books for parents and pastors to read — penetration, the endless ferment of the yeast.

And partnership — I do not mean simply a docile acceptance of the *status quo*. True partnership implies much more than that; it implies a recognition of the whole purpose of education, and of the part the State school does well, and of the part it does not do well, and of the part it cannot do at all.

It is partnership when the Church maintains independent schools, when they are better schools than the State schools, when they exercise a saving tension over against the monolith of the State school.

It is partnership when the Church, in her own religious teaching, understands more clearly what she should teach. Our failure has been that we have tried to teach 'religion' within the optional framework, as if God could be added at will, like whisky in an eggnog, to strengthen our teaching of history or English or whatever.

It is not a supplemental God or a supplemental religion that is the answer. Partnership means more than that; it means the creative fermenting conflict of a better idea and a fuller understanding of truth, with the partial truth and the half-understanding of the secular view.

But it requires that there be the closest relation, in time and circumstance, between what a child learns in the real school and what he learns in the Christian community. I repeat a basic principle: if you cannot learn about God and His will at the same time and in the same terms as you learn about history and politics and all the rest, you will never understand history very well or politics, and you will never understand God either.

Partnership does not require that a Sunday school teach history; it does require than a Sunday school teach youngsters how to understand history, and what it really is. Partnership does not require that the Church shall swagger into a university and damn the secularists with a faint reform; partnership does require that in the interior intellectual conflict of a university, the consequences of Christian faith shall be ardently and boldly presented. Partnership does not mean supplementation or the optional addition of God; it does not mean easy answers and closed systems; it means the introduction, in every way and at every stage, of the incarnate Lord, that men may see and understand more clearly their own natures and their hope.

But to do this would require a major shift of emphasis within our own body. Sunday schools now teach what parents should teach, because parents do not teach it, and because Sunday schools have often, following the secular pattern, tended to arrogate to themselves functions that can best be carried out only by and in a family. The rediscovery by the Church of the family as a basic unit is an exceedingly important event of recent time. It makes us hopeful that little by little the proper balance can be restored. If the parents and godparents will do their job of providing the natural Christian community for children, teaching them their prayers, reading the Bible with them, then the Sunday school, or its equivalent, can get on with the major job of teaching them how to understand history and science and how to be mature and radical citizens of a post-Christian democracy, able to choose freely and wisely the steps toward greater peace and justice.

This is what I mean by partnership. It is not a perfect way; there is no perfect way in an imperfect world; but this is where the battle lies, and we are not entitled to ask more than that.

It is a battle. The enemy is not the secularist or the secularist school. We fight not against principalities and powers. The enemy is a spirit, as much within the Church as outside it. And what is at stake is nothing less than the souls of the future. Against a spirit continually dragging man down in his own eyes, telling him he is deluded in his hope, telling him he really has no choices to make, telling him he is good because he is clever, telling him that the mediocre really is the excellent, telling him that there is no substance to his dream of heroic purity and heroic love — against that spirit the Christian stands and bears his sober witness to a knowledge of himself 'lower than the angels, yet to be crowned with glory and worship.' *Humility* and *hope* are the two great gifts that make a free society possible, that make it possible for men to be free, to take their necessary sides with passion and with gentleness. The world of the optional God is a world where men play at being angels, and only discover too late that the Devil is also a spirit. The world as God made it is not a world of angels — it is a world of mortals, who know they are lower than the angels but who have an invincible hope and an endless charity, and who know that Heaven and Hell depend on whether they use their freedom humbly and bravely. This world is the only world in which a free society is possible. This is the world for which we bear our honest witness. This is the world that God means our children to see.

IV

THE DIGNITY OF WORK

THE TITLE of this chapter is a quotation from a pamphlet issued by the World Council of Churches. The full quotation runs, 'In modern society the divine purpose of work is distorted and *the dignity of work is not respected*. This has been the cause of much of the present moral and spiritual chaos.' *

The two sentences are provocative to me. I like the phrase 'the dignity of work' very much indeed. I like rather less the somewhat aggrieved tone of the whole quotation. I like least of all the assumption that the loss of respect for work has been the cause of our present chaos. Indeed I think this is putting the cart before the horse. It is the moral and spiritual chaos of our time that has robbed work of its meaning and its joy.

This is not just quibbling. The facts are that for the majority of men in our society, their daily work is less and less satisfying and less and less meaningful. The very phrase itself, 'the dignity of work,' is a laughable and ridiculous phrase to them. What dignity is there

* *The Meaning of Work,* published by the Study Department of the World Council of Churches, September, 1950, p. 3 (italics mine).

to the fragmentary drudgery of the ordinary working man? There is none and he knows there is none.

Moralists can scold all they want to, and they do. Manufacturers' associations and columnists and business men and church assemblies all agree in scolding man because he does not work harder and does not take his work more seriously, because he does not perceive a dignity in his work. The last Lambeth conference solemnly reproached the world for not having more sense of divine vocation about its work, as if you could put on a sense of vocation like a pair of overalls.

I get uncomfortable at all this scolding. It's like losing your temper at a child because he gets the measles, except that the disease from which work suffers is far more deadly than any a child can get. It is a man's disease. It is the disease of godlessness, of a world and its work organized as if it made no difference whether there be a God or no. The chaos of a world without any idea of its own real nature is what empties our work and all we do of its meaning and dignity.

Start with the ordinary high-school boy in America today. A few months ago one of our popular magazines published an analysis of a cross section of American youth. It was no surprise to most of us, I am sure, that when the question was put about his ambition as far as a job was concerned, boy after boy answered that he did not much care what he did — business, medicine, the law — as long as it paid well so that he could retire early and then do what he really wanted to do. The tragedy of it lay not in his feeling that he wanted to make some money out of his job; the tragedy lay in the despair and joylessness of the whole prospect. Instead of looking at his work as a means of fulfillment, as a life that held meaning and promise and joy for him, as a job worth doing, he looked at it as something entirely separated from his real self and interests, as an activity inherently meaningless save only as a sort of temporary scaffolding to his life, or a flying buttress to support his personality from outside.

This is the predicament of probably a great majority of our brothers in the world. I think it is idle to reproach them for feeling that way. In point of fact it is probably the way they ought to feel, considering the jobs they are going to have to do.

Yet a man's work is too much a part of him to be dismissed as easily as that. Why is it that work is the problem it is to us?

I am going to suggest four reasons, I think in order of their importance. The first reason is that we are in the midst of a major revolution in the history of work. Men are being released more and more from the binding drudgery of the primary jobs, the immediate jobs, into secondary jobs, less immediate, more specialized, which are easier but far less satisfying in their content and in their social evaluation.

The revolution has gone farther in American life than anywhere else, and we are quite familiar with it. The dominant pattern, say a century ago, was the self-contained farmer or artisan, whose job was his way of life, who lived in immediate and direct contact with the major realities of life, who was relatively independent of other people as far as his major needs went, and who had all the securities and satisfactions that went with that autonomy. His was a hard job; but it was worth doing, for his whole life and his family's was tied up in it. He had stature in society, for he stood erect among his brothers, with clear meaning and value attaching to what he did.

The revolution in work has released him from the drudgery; it has provided him with money he did not have before; it has set him free from the immediate and imperative rhythms of nature that once held him. In return, it has required much of him. It has taken away the self-contained security and the natural satisfactions; it has involved him in a new dependence on a complicated economic machine; it has whittled down his job until it is no longer something he can immediately understand and evaluate. It has robbed him of the meaning he had; and now he must spend his time and energy trying to establish a new meaning, and wondering often whether there is any meaning to be found.

How sensitive we are to the problem of 'security' now. It is a vital problem; basically, however, it is not a money problem but a problem of meaning. The money security is essential, but it is the easiest of all securities to find. The basic security is contained in the answer to the question 'What is my job worth?'; and that question is increasingly difficult to answer because most of the jobs, in themselves, are not worth very much. Their meaning can be determined only by reference to a far larger whole; and man has not yet learned to think in those larger terms, or to find the social machinery to express his proper place in the larger whole.

This points to a second reason. The more you look at the larger wholes and the smaller jobs the more you see that two separate problems are involved. One is the problem of finding the meaning of your work not as an independent and primary producer but as a part of an organized process of which your job is only a fraction. The other is the problem of the value of the process itself.

Men can see the way to solve the first problem fairly readily. A young boy starting in a bank, say, or a railroad, can find meaning in his job right from the beginning. He is important, even in a minor way; he is contributing to a whole, and the whole makes sense, and he can see his way through and up. So he has a set of satisfactions given from the start, participation and hope and understanding.

The Horatio Alger myth of the boy who rises from track-walker to president of the railroad has a supremely important part to play in the divine economy. We laugh at the sentimentality of it, but actually that myth, which has leavened American life for generations, was one of the basic processes of our social health. It made it possible for men to adjust to an impersonal, complex, industrial reality, and to find a frame of reference that gave meaning to what they did.

The second problem is seen when you try to apply

the Horatio Alger myth to a job that is not really worth doing at all. There is where the rub comes. All pastors talk to many men about their jobs and become familiar with the typical psychosomatic patterns of dissatisfied, unsatisfied men who, on the surface, would seem to have everything life could give them. Their problem is not simply a problem of trying to find out what their job is or how to do it. They know that. Their problem is a far deeper one — they suspect the job is not worth doing anyway.

There is a profound and justified suspicion abroad in the world that much of our feverish and complicated activity is really only an elaborate way of keeping men off relief. We manufacture and we sell and we buy more junk per capita than any reasonable society can spiritually afford; and we know that; and we understand that in fact much of American industry is a sort of genial conspiracy to keep the money in circulation and keep producing and selling and buying so that everybody can have some sort of a job.

We do not like to say it that way. We are tempted, instead, to make a god out of 'Production' — indeed, more than once the National Association of Manufacturers has said, almost in so many words, that production is the end toward which all economic and industrial activity must move. We have adopted the senseless logic that more and more of things that are less and less important equals a higher standard of living. That is superstition and most sensible people know it is. But we are geared to the system nevertheless; our world would fall flat on its face economically if the endless torrent of soap and cars and bombs and perfume and plastic kitchen tables and radios and 1953 models of this and that were ever to stop. Some of it is good and worth producing. A lot of it is conspicuous and meretricious waste. That flood has washed away craftsmanship, it has destroyed our natural faith in excellence, it has debauched the radio, it has swept man away from his moorings until he is hopeless and confused, knowing it is imperative that the process go on, yet also knowing he must somehow restore a lost value to his own part in it.

There is no use telling such a man that he should find dignity or a sense of divine vocation in his work. He knows better than that. He knows that it would be only a very trivial and unimportant God, an optional God, who would be interested in such a job. He has sense enough for that; and he knows there are only two avenues of hope for him. He must either reach the point where the product does not matter, where all that matters is the money, the neutral power, or else he must find his real interest in something quite outside his work altogether. And you see both approaches, sometimes the two of them being used by the same person. When you progress, even in an unimportant industry, toward the top, you reach the point where you are dealing not with the actual work, its standards, its materials, its questionable social usefulness, but with power, neutral and real. At such a level of management, you escape from having to live day by day with the ethical vacuum of the process itself because you are now able to manipulate social realities. The modern corporation is a major factor in social welfare for instance. Through such agencies as the Community Chest, social work in the ordinary American city is to a large degree dependent on the will of management, which supports it. Management supports educational enterprises. It subsidizes and controls research. And at that level, if you reach it, you are exercising effective power, no matter how foolish the source of the money.

That is one form of the Horatio Alger myth; but it is possible only for the few, and the myth now significantly fails to convince the ordinary man. He is not sure that such a degree of social power is wise; he is certain that in any case it is not for him. And he is likely to take the other path: simply to agree that work is senseless drudgery and put up with it only so he can do what he really wants to do at the end of the day or at the end of his working life.

What sense is there in scolding him for that? He ought to do it, in justice to his own humanity. You cannot take a king-sized man and squeeze him into a matchbox. He will not fit, and he knows it. His problem is that he now has no alternative structure of value within which to find meaning. It is not a problem simply of leisure time; the vacuum is more than one of activity, it is a vacuum of value.

The third reason for our discontent lies still deeper in the structure of our life. I have already stated that all of us have had to come to terms with the industrial process by which we gain our daily bread. We do, by various myths — free enterprise (which is a good myth), ownership (which is a bad myth because it is misleading), the myth of production for its own sake (which is a senseless myth), and so on. But we are fumbling for a more fundamental solution than we have yet found. And that search is profoundly reflected in our uneasiness and discontent.

Let me go back again to the revolution in work. The significant aspect of the American industrial revolution is not a matter of size or productivity or technical skill. It is rather what one of our economists calls 'a new concept of organizing men for work.' * The meaningful unit is no longer the man working, or many men working. It is a larger and impersonal unit, the *plant*, which alone makes sense. Men are but fractional parts of the plant. Whether they are apprentices at the bottom or presidents at the top, they are still fractions. It is the plant alone that holds the secret of their meaning. The parts are interchangeable, and they must be; the craftsman is an anachronism and a luxury; it is not desirable that any man stick out too much as an individual because in the end his real function and status will be decided by the plant.

This anonymity and interchangeability is of course the basic secret of efficiency and of high production. It is what makes it possible for us to win wars, among

* Peter F. Drucker, 'The New Society 1. Revolution by Mass Production,' a reprint from Harper's Magazine, September 1949, p. 3.

other things. It is an achievement of stupendous industrial importance. If it could be limited to that, it would be no particular problem.

But in the natural order of things, a man's work is the chief way in which he finds his status and dignity in society. The community is involved because to have a community means being able to say what a man does and to have some idea of what his work is worth. The bony structure of a community is largely made up of men's jobs and their values. And in proportion as the plant becomes the value-giver, to that proportion the plant is urged toward becoming the community; indeed by its very nature it must.

The plant exercises social power more and more, because it wields the effective power in society. The plant collects funds for social and charitable purposes; it organizes study and reading groups for its executives; it plans social activities for its workers; it prescribes social behavior for its executives' wives; it provides more and more inclusive schemes for the welfare of its employees; it begins to function more and more as a natural community because it is irresistibly driven to it by the logic of its own being.

We do not have to face it now, but before too long we shall have to face the basic question of the progressive reorganization of society around the industrial community. There are many signs of the times, not dramatic, not important in themselves necessarily, but cumulative. Labor plays a new role in industry when it will force its way, or be invited, into management more and more. Anyone can buy stock. Anyone can own a corporation. By the same token power is there to be seized and used; and the fact of the new community will arise more and more, and it will have to be faced and mastered.

I do not pretend to foresee how it will come, or to prejudge it. I know that it is not good for a society to have its real power isolated from its political and social controls, and that is our situation in part. The political realities and the industrial realities are out of phase with each other in our world, and that imbalance cannot last.

But the heart of the problem is not what form the new community will take. The heart of the problem is the moral structure of the community. Either man is the master of his work, or its slave; and whether he will be the master or not depends not on industrial or economic factors but on theological factors. Man is a theological problem. Work is a theological problem. And an impersonal industrial community simply cannot create meaning or assign value.

To say that is to come to the last reason why there is a problem of work in our society. Work cannot be understood or evaluated without reference to God. A society with an optional God simply cannot make sense out of its work. The secular experiment, the revolution, in America has been precisely the attempt to define the good life entirely in terms of producing, buying, and selling. It is the 'egoism' of the industrial society, which arrogates to itself, sucks up into itself the value-giving functions of society, that has cheated man out of one of his fundamental joys.

It is a benevolent monster. The story of America is the story of the prodigal richness of this secular experiment. Christians are sometimes beguiled into being sentimental about industrial society. We look back at old times and long for the great simplicities of a simpler time, in a more personal world where dependences were more direct and obligations and pleasures more immediate. It is a significant nostalgia, and a well-intentioned one; but it is still sentimental.

Or we are likewise beguiled into another sentimentality, when we adjudge the secular world as a 'materialist' world and long for a more 'spiritual' quality of life. This is also quite unreal. Christianity is not a particularly spiritual religion; in fact it is rather suspicious of spirituality; it is a sacramental religion, very down-to-earth, very materialistic when it deals with the material, very aware of the fallen angels, very aware that the Devil is also a spirit. The antithesis to the secular, industrial society is not a clerical, ethical society, where prayer and art will take the place of machines and plants. The true antithesis is between a society that has no God to whom it may offer its handiwork, and a society to which the act of oblation is the final and concluding act of the whole inventive process. Not more churches and fewer factories; but more churches in the factories, in at least a symbolic sense.

Let us remind ourselves always that the secular

world is a good world, and that the flood of invention and technical industrial skill has been by and large an immensely good and great gift to the world. The creative skill of America has been found there. The heroic stories of American life have been written there.

There are the stories of the railroads, of the mines, of the motor car, of the airplane, as they have been worked out against the vast distances and the technical poverty of an earlier America — a man would be an insufferable snob if he did not warm and thrill at the greatness of them. Somewhere someone wrote that 'man is at his worst when he is pitted against his brother man — he is at his best when he is pitted against nature.' The story of industrial America has been a story of man at his best, opening the way, as far as the natural gifts can do it, to a richer and fuller life for all of us.

But the monster is still a monster, blind and pitiless, willing to serve any idol, any master, who will capture him. And to let the monster erect itself into its own god is disaster.

Just consider what the claims of that idolatry are. It requires the deliberate adoption of the mediocre because of its own urgent requirement of what can be produced at the lowest cost. This means not only the increasing loss of craftsmanship; it means also the increasing stifling of invention. The mass-produced automobile, for instance, which has been an extraordinarily liberating force in our society, at the same time is a monument of mediocrity. The deliberate suppres-

sion of technical possibilities; the deliberate fashion-
ing of cars far less efficient and far less safe than they
could be, because of the logic of a mass market; and the
consequent debasing of the very standards of excellence and truth themselves — those are the real price
tags on an automobile. The bargain is very likely a
good one, taken by itself; but the cumulative effect
of the principle I rather think is exceedingly dangerous. But the idol requires mediocrity.

The idol requires what it calls 'practicality.' That is
to say, it contains within itself the standards of what is
important and right, and therefore it requires conformity to those standards. For example, deep in the
nature of true scientific investigation is the principle
of disinterestedness. Before science asks the question
'What is this good for?' she asks, 'What is this and
where does it lead?' The more society insists that what
is studied or learned must be what society has an immediate use for, the more she stifles the fundamental
curiosity at the heart of all learning. A subsidized investigation in a laboratory for a specific project is an
excellent and nourishing thing, as long as there is no
question but what it is a side show and not in the main
tent. But to the degree that science is equated with
mere technicism, to just that degree does the fountain
of true science run dry. It is never safe to ask the question 'What is this good for?' if there is not an unques-
tioned assumption that it may turn out to be good for
nothing, and that it does not matter much anyway.
America is very proud of its technical skill; we some-

times confuse it with what we call 'science.' They are quite different, technically and philosophically, and the guarantee of success in one does not necessarily carry over to the other. Contrary to popular superstition, scientists do not spend most of their time testing tooth powder or endorsing cigarettes.

The idol requires many sacrifices. It has no great opinion of that most insecure person in our society, the artist; it has not too much concern with the teacher except in so far as he can train technicians or indoctrinate a docile public; it does not care for the eccentric or the individual; it really does not care too much for man — this concrete individual. As long as he remains comfortably in the abstract, as a predictable mass appetite or mass force, he is allowed to remain. Like an Indian on a reservation, he is tolerated as long as he does not interfere with the orderly colonizing of the country. But in all his angular individualism he is more nuisance than he is worth.

We see this most clearly in the principle of interchangeability in the mass production plant where, because of the nature of the process, it is insisted that man remain in the abstract, an integer to be dealt with only in impersonal combination.

The idol has its sacred symbols, and its creeds and hymns. The myth of an automatic 'progress' — that because we can do something this year which we could not do last year, therefore we are better off this year than we were last year — that is the controlling myth. The idol has its shibboleth of 'a better standard of living,' which must be pronounced by anyone seeking to enter its circles.

We could play infinite variations on this theme. It is a profound illustration of an inviolable principle, that we pay for what we get. We get a great deal from a technical, industrial society. But the price is very high. Actually we began to suspect that the price is nothing less than man himself.

My years as a student and the beginning years of my ministry were years dominated by the most calamitous sign of the cost of an industrial society — mass unemployment. The price of our particular social idolatry was written clearly and shockingly. We had taken it very much for granted that man was the gainer by all this prodigious process, and then suddenly it began to occur to us that, actually, man was in the greatest peril. To quote Peter Drucker again, industrial man 'is like a blindfolded man in a strange room, playing a game of which he does not know the rules; and the prize at stake is his own happiness, his own livelihood and even his own life.' *

Man's work, which in every society had been one of the great means of giving him stature and meaning and dignity, now had failed of its primary purpose. It had promised that he would gain the whole world; yet he apparently had lost his own soul in the process. He was rootless and irrational; he was suddenly the victim of the idol he had thought to worship.

* Peter F. Drucker, *The Future of Industrial Man,* New York, The John Day Company, 1942, p. 28.

The consequence of that discovery was no less critical than the discovery. The consequence was the counter-revolution which has swept through society like a fire — the determination that this must not happen again, the determination that the system shall be for man and not man for the system. I think some of the indications of that counter-revolution are of paramount significance.

One is the change in the inner dynamics of the labor movement. Men still sometimes talk about 'radicalism,' or the 'irrepressible conflict' between capital and labor, or the warfare between the opposing interests of 'the worker' and 'the boss.' Those ancient tintypes are museum pieces. The most conservative force in American industry today is the labor movement. Apart from a few individuals and a few areas of special pressures, the old voice of the self-conscious, fighting labor movement is almost gone. It is not conflict or the rights of labor that are in question; it is *security*. It is the question of how to manage this monster so that there is something for everybody and assurance about tomorrow. It is quite self-conscious. In government, in industry, in politics, in labor, the key words are words such as 'welfare' and 'security.'

It is good that this should be. The first requirement of work is that it should give stature and meaning to the workers. It is good that man should regain mastery over the process that feeds him. It is idle to complain that we are hypnotized by security, or to blame it on the Communists, or to pine for older and more independent days. The real question is what lies ahead. It is, basically, the question whether man himself can master his industrial society without reference to God. It is easy enough, given the will and sufficient ingenuity, to work out the controls that will harness the system — the controls of economic security, the controls of labor-management negotiation, and all the myriad mechanisms that preserve the delicate balance of an industrial society. Man himself is the ambiguous element. This immense impulse, felt everywhere in the world, to re-establish man on the throne and restore his primacy in the world — all this vast tide of human reassertion, of the most profound significance politically — comes in the end to the timeless and unhurried question, 'What is man?'

Berdyaev said 'Man without God is no longer man.' * It is this profoundly disquieting discovery that is the real point of anxiety for us in our world. If it is true, then all the rest of our fight for justice and security will hang on our answer to the root question. If man and his work is basically a theological question, then the answer to that question must be basically a theological answer. Indeed, the Marxist answer, which is the most vivid one our world has yet proposed, is basically a theological one (but it is not very good theology, if only for the reason that it deifies the very

---

* Nicholas Berdyaev, *The End of Our Time,* New York, Sheed and Ward, 1933, p. 54. This whole chapter, 'The End of the Renaissance,' strikes me as an acute and classic analysis of this point.

contradiction in society itself). To a people who have lost their basic satisfactions because they have tried to live as if a full stomach were the answer to every problem, Marxism offers only the consolation that such is the inner secret of reality. The Church has another certainty; she remembers One who stood alone, confronted with the very secret and prize of earthly power itself, and said 'Man does not live by bread alone.'

I rather think that there, in the Wilderness, is where the Church's answers to the problem of work are to be found. They are going to be pretty basic answers, if they are to be real at all.

We are far too easily given — indeed it is part of the professionalizing of religion — to feel that all will come right if only we can baptize the baby, so to speak. All sorts of church activities come under that heading, all the way from Buchmanism with its program of converting the tycoons, to the Catholic Trade Union, or Industrial Chaplaincies. All of these are largely attempts to modify or adapt to an underlying industrial reality without seriously thinking of changing it. As far as they go they are good. It is no sin to convert a businessman. But these activities are not going to change the fundamental dynamics at all, good and wholesome though they may be. This does not mean that we should not engage in them; it simply means that an industrial society cannot be manipulated from outside, as if it were an atomic pile.

'Penetration,' again, is the word I want. I would venture to say that the minister who works with his hands in the factory, or who rises to power in a labor union, will have far more authority to speak than he would in a chaplain's office. Certainly the work of the laity is here. In the ferment and conflict of industry itself, in the use of the social power controlled by industry, in the formulation of standards by which industry is guided, in the making of the laws by which industry is governed — these are the areas where clear and decisive Christian witness is required. And by and large the clergy will not have too much to say directly, nor should they.

Indirectly, the clergy are likely to have everything to say. For in the slow, momentous years of this revolution, what will be at stake all the time will be the truth about man himself. Not 'How can we guard the security of this present man?' but rather the deeper question 'What does his true security consist of?' Not 'How shall we see that he has a steady wage?' but 'How shall we restore dignity to his work?' It is a good thing that society has determined to set man at the top; in the relativity of a world without God, however, 'top' and 'bottom' alike are meaningless words. The greatest security the State gives may in the end be a prison house. It has been so before.

It will be with the words that the clergy will wrestle most. That lovely archaism, 'vocation,' will be the one we shall examine first, a word which comes to us instinct with Christian meanings, but which has dwindled until it means no more than whatever pigeonhole of usefulness a psychologist or a personnel man puts us in. 'Vocation' implies one who calls; and an optional God is dumb. 'Vocation' implies the freedom to answer the call with a whole heart; and for the vast masses of men where is that freedom? We have whittled that word down until it is no more than a synonym for the accidental crevice in which we lodge. We have forgotten that at the root there is only one vocation, which calls all men — the vocation to be holy and to offer themselves and their work to Him. Unless the whole of life be offered, and all of us in our accidental roles, the individual dignity of vocation is archaic and meaningless. I should not debase God by urging a man trapped in a meaningless job to call the job his 'vocation.' His vocation is to be a whole man under God. This is the use of the word that needs to be recovered.

We shall wrestle with the words; and we need also to find again the lost unity of prayer and work. That is partly a matter of leisure time. As all work demands less and less of ourselves, and gives less and less in return, our center of gravity shifts. Work becomes a wretched necessity for forty hours a week, endurable because it sets us free for really interesting avocations that are completely separate from our work. It would be a poor and uninventive Church that did not seize this new freedom and rescue it from the tavern and the sodden emptiness of the debauched Saturdays and Sundays of our time. I mean hobbies, and I mean teaching people how to read, and I mean the rediscovery of nature, and I mean the re-creation of the family group. I sometimes wonder what in the world we build our parish houses for? Are they only for women's teas and children's classes? There they stand, half-used, and all around us there are people wishing they had some place they could go to work and to do something interesting.

But it is more than the problem of leisure time. It is the rediscovery of an ancient wholeness to life that we are really after. To work and to pray are almost the same act; it is hard to tell where one starts and the other stops. How marvelously well some pastors have discovered that, and what it has meant to all people who have found the lost wholeness and the lost dignity in the rediscovery of the oblation of work and the work of prayer.

For a man's work is not only a harsh necessity. It is that, and for legions of imprisoned humanity it can be no more than that now. But the myth of the Fall misleads in one respect; we sometimes forget that although man was cast out of the Garden, he was not cast out of God's world. The world and its work are still God's. We are tormented by a remembrance of a time out of time when the pain of work was not part of our life. Yet there is a hope greater than the memory — the hope that the freedom of the exile from innocence may in the end be a partnership that crowns man with glory.

I quote again from Dr. Oldham, 'The Christian view goes much deeper than the mere assertion . . . that unless men work the race cannot survive. It is an affirmation that work is inherent in God's purpose for man and an essential expression of man's nature as created in the image of God the Creator . . . work can acquire a real meaning in the Christian sense only when it is done in a framework and context in which the Christian meaning of life as a responsibility to God and service to men is not frustrated and denied.' *

We read that and we agree profoundly — *Laborare est orare* — and we remember the Workman and the somber words 'Man does not live by bread alone.'

* J. H. Oldham, *Work in Modern Society*, London, S.C.M. Press, 1950, pp. 49–50.

V

FREEDOM AND INDIVIDUALITY

AT ONE point in the preparation of these lectures I sat reading and listening in the back of my mind to the St. John Passion which was being played on the record player in the next room. Suddenly and quite vividly it came to me, as I suppose it does to all of us over and over again, that the real heart of our faith and the real heart of life itself for all of us post-Christians is found in the Passion of Christ. That timeless and absolute story, the story to which all other stories of suffering and glory are relative, must be close to the innermost and most precious secret of humanity. No matter how men believe it or do not believe it, no matter how well we remember it, it is in our bloodstream. It established for us a totally new dimension of pain. The wounds in hands and feet and side somehow have changed for us the way we look at our wounds. The injustice of the Cross became a new standard by which we appraised our own injustices. The Cross itself came into our language to illuminate our own pilgrimage. The love of Calvary lighted and purified our own love.

For the pagan as well as the Christian, for the humanist and the secularist quite as much as for the disciple, the Passion has been the central core of the whole revelation. For the pagan understood as well as the Christian that it was not enough merely to know the truth in abstract terms. Truth had finally to be lived out. The man of good will, with his natural intimations of morality, had to become himself more than teacher or observer or philosopher or friend — he had himself to realize his knowledge in the fire of a devoted and consecrated will. Socrates emerged from the cave to see the sun; and forever after a compulsion was laid upon him: not a compulsion to love, because that was a deeper knowledge still to come which only the Cross could teach, but an awakening to the obligation of light to which the Cross, when it came, was the fulfillment.

Truth had to become a story told, acted — and in the world of our inheritance, the Cross is that story. Deep called to deep; to the humanist as to the disciple, the story rang true. St. Paul was quite right in saying that the Cross was foolishness and a stumbling block; so was Socrates' hemlock; so is it always when nobility meets necessity, when love and sin intersect. In worldly eyes the Cross is always foolishness; but at a deeper level the pagan saw as the disciple did, that wise or foolish, fact or dream, the Cross was a necessary dimension without which man could not understand himself or his pain.

The controversy between pagan and Christian lay not in the Cross but in the Resurrection, where it lies now. The Passion is universal; it is the possibility of the Church and the Kingdom that is always in doubt.

Why is it that the Cross casts that universal spell over all men? The answer seemed to me to lie in the heart of man himself. His struggle with the world outside himself and inside himself — what does it signify? His endless awareness of a necessity to choose, his persistent search for a self that has only been half-given to him, his gnawing discontent with the conditions of his own existence, and his restless dreams which drive him into unceasing improvisations of what he calls a better world and a better self — what do these things mean? He is unfinished. He has a story to write with his life that he has never heard, nor does he know the end of it. Plato again — 'Something there is which every soul desires; that it is he knows, but what it is he knows not, nor does he know the way.'

Back to the very beginning it has been so with us. This absurd, self-conscious little dot in the universe — what is the meaning of this ferment and judgment within? So much a part of the nature that surrounds us, so deeply dominated by the dark tides of the flesh, so imprisoned by necessity, yet still aware that 'I' stands over against 'that' or 'thee,' and that in some inescapable urgency I must decide the issues myself. It is 'I' and not 'they' who in the end will choose. There is shame and glory in the very tissues of life themselves. What do these things mean?

It is to this in man that the Cross speaks, because the Cross is the story of freedom. It is the story written by the one free Man we know. If it is not a true story, if there be no first day of the week, then it is a story of infinite pathos and tragedy; and so then also is the enigmatic freedom that flickers and flames in a man's heart. But deep still calls to deep; here, enthroned at the heart of life, is the free Man; and in some extraordinary way we find ourselves explained and justified in Him. Even if the end is tragedy, foolishness, still the writing of the story of the Passion in every man's heart is the only way to peace and to a secure selfhood for him.

These two gifts, freedom and individuality, are the two central gifts of the Cross to the world; and they are so because they answer the deepest questions in humanity itself.

Once again, let us remember that these are not 'religious' truths. The Cross is not a 'religious' fact. Sometimes I look at the brassware on our altars, or the casual irreverence in the way we sometimes cross ourselves, and I marvel at how so universal a symbol has dwindled until it signifies no more than a trademark of self-righteousness. The Cross is part of humanity; it is the massive central symbol to which all life conforms, believing or not believing. What is important to say now is that the precise crisis of our culture at this moment is the deliberate attempt to choke out of man that part of him to which the Cross speaks and which the Cross illuminates. The attempt will not succeed, because this is truth with which we are dealing, and truth is God's and not ours. But the Christian who tries to understand what his apostolate is in our time will not understand it until he sees that the actual crisis is a crisis in freedom and in individuality, and that these gifts are what are actually at stake.

The eternal barbarian who is standing at the threshold of the world waiting for an unguarded door so he may slip in — who is he? A Church that takes the parable of the first century as an allegory, as I suggested we are tempted to do, identifies the barbarian in first-century terms, as if history repeated itself. On the contrary, I think we are dealing with a baptized barbarian, a post-Christian barbarian, who is in the family. Who is he? The barbarian in our culture is the one to whom freedom and individuality are ridiculous. He is the one to whom it is meaningless to speak of the Cross as a story of freedom. Indeed he is the one to whom the very writing of a story of a man's life is a ridiculous proposal. To him all notion of a real choice or a real contingency is impossible; life is a laboratory report of what happens to you; decision is no more than the line of least resistance; personality is the sum total of the accidental and whimsical chances of an uncaring fate, like the baubles on a Christmas tree decorated by a madman; principle signifies no more than prejudice; selfhood is a thumbprint of society; liberty is an alms from a legislature.

Now, as always, over against the eternal barbarian stands the civilized man, the child of the Cross, to whom the precarious adventure of selfhood and society itself is always a story of the particular and the individual man choosing his way into selfhood, choosing his way toward excellence, and weaving civilized life as he goes in the very fabric of his arduous choices. The civilized man is the one to whom freedom and individuality are the most precious things he knows. For them he is prepared to sacrifice all other gifts, if need be life itself, for he knows that to gain the whole world is an empty bargain if the world in the end is to be a prison house for him. For the sake of those twin gifts he has built into the structure of the State great defenses against arrogance and against the crushing absolutes of political power. He guards with the greatest care what he calls the 'rights' of the individual — the right to speak, the right to a free trial by his peers — not because the individual is worthy of those protections, not because he thinks the bad man is really a good man, but because he is a man and has what we stumblingly call an 'inalienable right' to these things.

He maintains the greatest vigilance over the little store of wisdom he has learned and over the transmission of it, because he knows that imperfect as our knowledge is and imperfect as our freedom is in seeking it, still our hope is in an ever-advancing and ever-widening circle of light. He wants to know, and he wants other people to know, all they can know; for he is sure that tyranny lurks in the prescription of truth, in the limitation of truth, by any society.

He knows that there is a purification of excellence that can come no other way, for freedom is nothing else than the endless search for a more excellent way. So he is not willing ever to stop with what is possible; he will not ever absolutize what he has done so far; there is an inner scourge that drives him in his daily work, to guide him, so he is convinced, daily nearer God.

The confrontation of this civilized man by the eternal barbarian is the actual crisis of our time. It is to this crisis that the Church speaks.

Think back for a moment over the specific areas in which this is so clearly seen. In the political area, where the focus now falls on the State and statism, the crisis begins to take form. In our society the massive safeguard against the encroachment of the State has always been the dike of liberalism, sometimes a party, sometimes a self-conscious group, but always there, so that we could comfortably assume that behind that dike there was a safe harbor where men could rebuild their strength as they needed it for the defense of freedom and the individual. This liberalism was an attitude nourished by the legacy of Christendom. And the refusal of liberalism to accept men as a means, the refusal even to speak of men as Man, lest in this way the particular sense of selfhood be lost in an abstraction, this refusal was the historic check within the body of Western society that stood against every attempt to absolutize. Like the wave in the swift-running water, society curled back against itself in that refusal. And we were fat and comfortable; like Mr. Podsnap, we had a 'glorious Constitution' better than any other, and beneath it the freedom of man was secure.

What we did not see was that liberalism is a derivative, an inheritance; that it could not reproduce itself; that it was basically a matter not of politics at all but of theology. Left to itself, liberalism serves barbarism quite as aptly as it does the civilized man. There is only one direction for liberalism to take, when it has lost its certainty about God, and that is totalitarianism. When the men in society themselves cease to be the center and the end, when the given fact of their freedom and the eternal struggle for selfhood and individuality is dimmed and lost, when the roots in the Cross are cut, then liberalism subtly changes its character. It becomes a species of absolutism, a rationalist absolutism, in which the Christian search for a free society is forgotten, and the older assertion of the 'best' society, or what is best for society, reappears.

This is theory, or it could have been mistaken for theory, were it not for the political history of the past thirty years or so. We remember the bleak commentary of Einstein on Nazi Germany, of how he had looked to all the liberal institutions in German society to stand against totalitarianism — the universities, business, the newspapers — and one by one they all capitulated, and finally, in the end, there was only the Church, which he had neglected, left to stand against the State. How that same pattern of the disintegration of liberalism has repeated itself, in country after country — a new barbarism arising in the very heart of a generation that had prided itself on reaching the summit of the liberal spirit.

We in America should guard ourselves well against

taking our own liberalism for granted. We need to remember that we have not yet faced the issue of totalitarianism within our own body; we should beware lest we be self-righteous, and we must not be stupid enough to suppose that the amiable prejudices of a comfortable people will guard the inner citadel of freedom. The 'American way of life' can be absolutized and deified quite as readily as any other tyrant. We need now, more than we have ever needed it in our history, the native Christian skepticism about the State and about all absolutes. A pale, liberal prejudice against despotism is completely ineffectual; and people know it; and they see the rise of totalitarianism all around them, even within their own hearts — most of all within their own hearts — and they are afraid that the liberal world is a vanished world altogether, and that liberalism is a luxury fit only for easy times.

So it might be, if it were not for the Cross. We say to one another that we should not bring politics into the pulpit; and we are right, if by politics we mean partisan advantage or passing expedience. But to carry that principle to the point that some carry it, to suppose that the Church is neutral on the basic issues of political life, to suppose that the Church should confine itself to technical 'religion,' is to commit the sin of optionalism. There is no neutrality in Christianity as far as the State is concerned. The Christian attitudes toward man and the State are not matters of fashion or prejudice at all; they are matters of principle that are rooted in reality. God made man free, and an end in himself under God. And the only unswerving barrier to the totalitarian and barbarian spirit lies there. And we should teach people about these matters.

The same vivid confronting of the barbarian spirit is found in other fields of life. I am always very sensitive, for example, in anything I say about education, to the charge that what the Church is really pleading for is to turn the clock back. Sometimes I think we sound that way. We sound as if we were trying to re-establish an older world, a gentler and more comfortable world, where a 'gentleman's education' was possible and relevant, and where the public school or college would do the Church's work for us.

Actually that is not what is in question at all. What is important is the appearance of a new idea, or the re-appearance of an old one, of man himself and the nature and purpose of his knowledge. The difference between education and indoctrination is the difference between man as an end and man as a means. Any society that in its educational system adopts as its end the adjustment or conditioning or training of a child to fit that given society and no other is not educating but indoctrinating. What matters there is not the freedom and individuality of the child; what matters is the orderly functioning of the society. This is a baptized barbarism. The leaven that Christianity introduced into education was exactly the opposite of this. It was the perception that one of the principal ends of education must be to teach a child how to be free, how to make judgments and to take sides, how to reach and find a standard of judgment quite outside the society and its scheme of values altogether.

The quarrel of the Church and the school is at this point, and it is a basic quarrel. It goes beyond 'indoctrination' into the very nature of human life itself, and into the nature of truth. What is at stake is not gentility or humane values themselves. What is at stake is the very persistence of the idea of the free individual.

The barbarous man, the mass man, is the man obsessed with the superstition of science. Both in school and in industry, he is the man who has found a substitute for freedom and for the whole precarious, difficult enterprise of being a person. The old framework of religion has been disproved, he believes; the old wrestling of conscience, the old agonies of choice of right and wrong have become anachronistic. What he calls 'science' has, he feels, eliminated these old mythologies. He adopts the new mythologies of automatic progress, of technical advancement. He tells himself that he is better off than he was last year because he has newer techniques than last year. He has discovered how to mold the human spirit, by tempting, by frightening, by lying and bullying. He is ignorant and he imagines that these techniques are new, and that they have supplanted the older ones of examination and reflection and choice.

This obsession with mass techniques, with conforming pressures from outside a personality, rather than the far harder evoking of response from within a personality, this superstition about determinism that masquerades as 'science' — this is barbarism at work.

The response of Christianity to it is certainly not one of abdication. It is perfectly futile to say that the answer to it is to have less science in education. The enemy is not too much knowledge but too little knowledge. The so-called 'scientific attitude' in the mass man of our society is really no more than learned ignorance. He trusts blindly in a science he has no pretense of understanding; he is willing to be manipulated by technical processes with which he does not care to be too troubled. All of the vivid and particular and personal relationships tend to fade away; community ceases to be of concern to him; brutality sweeps in. He relishes only the creature comforts which the monster brings him, and waves away responsibility and freedom and individuality altogether.

It may be that nothing less than the disintegration of his whole society will shake that terrible complacency of the mass man. When he discovers, in Ortega y Gasset's phrase,* how much else must also be kept alive if the spirit of science is to live, then he may rally from his ignorance. When he discovers that in the end there is no chance of neutrality, that man will have what kind of self he chooses, and what kind of society he chooses and no other, he may look again and more deeply at the nature of truth and the obligation it

---

* José Ortega y Gasset, *The Revolt of the Masses,* New York, W. W. Norton, 1932, p. 91. 'Has any thought been given to the number of things that must remain active in men's souls in order that there may continue to be "men of science" in real truth?'

imposes. Whitehead said 'Man does not discover in order to know, he knows in order to discover.' It is the endlessly receding horizon of freedom that is the background of all truth. Knowledge does not solve the problem of choice; it only intensifies it; it only opens the way to wider and wiser choice, or else turns back on itself in destruction.

Well, this is only to say that the real crisis of our time is internal. There is an internal barbarism, which attacks in the most sensitive areas of all, freedom and self-hood, and violates the most cherished values of our culture.

The Christian may well be thankful for any defense of those values. We should not be too scornful of the humanist and the secularist; they may not have the reasons we have for our faith, but we need one another. However, it remains true that the post-Christian humanist needs the Christian more than the Christian needs him, because the 'is' comes before the 'ought' — reality breeds values and supports them. The Christian believes in freedom and the individual not just because he likes free individuals but because the nature of the universe is such that it moves toward free individuality as the end. Every man looks at his own native intuitions of freedom, and he sees that he must come to terms with them, either to accept them and the heroic vocation they imply, or else reject them as absurd and irrational, and quench all the personal fire of life.

To every man the Christian faith offers a solid and

authentic answer. It bids him accept his fragmentary surmise. It says to him 'Your freedoms are indivisible and they are real. Your life, your self, is not a passive clay. It is a dialogue with God. It is a story you shall write with your choices.'

To the question 'How can this freedom be real?' the Christian faith has no easy answer. We are not a very theoretical people. We start with what we know, the ache and itch of freedom within our own spirits, the impulse to win the same freedom for others, and to respect it in them. And we ask what kind of reasonable universe it would be that could contain this contingency, this freedom.

Certainly not the limited and determined universe of a purely natural faith. There could be no freedom in that machine. It could only be a universe in which personal relationships are supreme, in which free choices, which are at least as real as time is, fit somehow into the fundamental purpose of the Creator. Time was when the simple history of the Bible gave us a clue to this universe, but we have gone beyond that. But, as Butterfield says, 'What was unique about the ancient Hebrews was their historiography rather than their history.' * Their history was the history of a hundred nations. What set them apart incomparably was the way they interpreted and used the vicissitudes of time. The somber and magnificent response of the prophets to disaster; the profound insights into suffer-

* Herbert Butterfield, *Christianity and History*, London, G. Bell, 1949, p. 73.

ing; the relentless acceptance of guilt instead of the querulous fault-finding with the gods that is the substance of so much pagan history — it is these insights, penetrating into a history behind history, seeing a Divine will moving and building in the shadows behind the scaffolding of human events, that open the way to a greater account of God's way with His Creation.

For what we read in this greater chronicle is the story of God in His love calling this cosmos out of nothing; implanting in it and communicating to it His laws; stage by stage evoking from it a response to Him so that at no level is the Creation simply clay in His hands but is living with His life and is as close to Him and in a sense as large a part of His life as a story written by an earthly writer; filling the cosmos with His purpose; at each level giving it what of His purpose and will it can receive and respond to; but always relentlessly moving toward the perfect end that will ultimately explain and make right all that has gone before.

The doctrine of creation, truly seen, is never the doctrine of an act or a series of acts; it always penetrates behind the acts to the will and purpose that animates them. Creation is far more analogous to the work of a writer than to the work of a potter; it is still closer to the work of a father who seeks from his children not simply existence or obedience but a free recognition of and response to his love. Even an earthly father is mysterious at times to his children, when he holds back from coercion and patiently bides their mistakes. The children are often not conscious of him or his love; they take his care for granted; they are occasionally mystified by his refusal to make them do what he wills. They are sometimes even rebellious against the fact that he holds them, as he does himself, to a common standard that is hard for them to attain; and they rebel against his pain when they do not attain it. But in the end, if all goes well, there is evoked from them a relationship far more enduring and far more glorious than the easier alternatives had looked. The free and loving response, the return, fulfilled and worked out in another life, of the will and purpose in the father's heart — that is the prize of earthly parenthood.

I imagine that the creative action of God is more akin to that than to any other we know. As far as I can see, there is no other doctrine of creation that can explain man's ambiguous and unique consciousness. If God has cast the temporal process out of Himself, so to speak, it must be that in the end it is to return to Him, that He may be all and in all. And it is at the level of human consciousness that creation first reaches the capacity to respond in reason and will, and so begin the fulfillment of the temporal process.

I say again, I do not know any other doctrine of creation that can explain and justify this trembling, awkward sense of freedom in man's self-consciousness. It may be waste material; it may be to no purpose, all this equipment for prayer and heroic choice and sacrifice that man carries around with him. But if this is a coherent universe, and if a single purpose animates it all, then it is to its highest point — the life of Jesus — that we look for a clue to that purpose. But the purpose is there at every point, vivifying and valuing, pressing toward its fulfillment even though at the moment it may hardly be seen or recognized at all. This is what the real truth of the evolutionary theory comes to. And this is the secret of historiography, as the prophets first saw. It is this that makes it possible for men to discern a rational universe and to gauge themselves in the scheme of that universe.

In Christian terms, I suppose this is what St. John means when he writes, 'In the beginning was the Word and the Word was with God, and the Word was God . . . All things were made by him; and without him was not any thing made that was made.' 'At the heart of all creation is the meaningful will and purpose of the Father; He gives that purpose and intention to all created things, indeed without it they would not exist.' Without a rational doctrine of creation, real freedom would be inconceivable. Without the Cross, freedom would be impossible.

The more a man explores the substance of his manhood, this dialogue with God, this story he is writing, the more surely he comes to the final question, 'What is to keep my freedom from being simply chaos and destruction for myself?'

And the answer is that the only peace for man is in the Father's will. It is in God's service that our freedom will be found, and our vivid and united self. All the fragmentary selves, all the separate wills of the incomplete man find their unity and their fulfillment in the obedience of the Cross.

Christianity offers no easy, neat, managed universe. It offers no social absolute. It offers no easily molded impersonality into which a man may sink himself, caring for nothing, believing in nothing, hoping for nothing.

Christianity offers only sharp and clear selfhood, worked out in a myriad choices. It offers a man only the chance to disengage himself from the whole. It offers him only the freedom to write what story he will with his life. It offers him pain, and a dazzling bright light on the steps he takes in this life.

Christianity requires all his freedom in return. The medieval knight took this vow to his lord, 'Before Him to whom this shrine is holy, I will be faithful and true to my prince; I will love all that he loves; I will shun all that he shuns; and never of my will or power do ought that may be hurtful to him.' That is the vow every free man takes, if he accepts his freedom at all.

The immeasurable gift of God is that in this bondage, and in it alone, is man set free from the bondage of this world, from the tyranny of power, and from the crushing darkness of the faceless and anonymous. This bondage is what makes it possible for man to recognize and cherish his brother. It is what makes it possible for a man to be himself.

VI

THE CHURCH AND THE KINGDOM

IN MANY ways, the most difficult and complicated part of the Church's task is part not really of this task at all, but of the preparation of ourselves for the task. What I refer to is the weakening of our own interior witness and integrity by the alien spirits of the world. I remember reflecting on this at the time the lectures on which this book is based were being delivered. I had to return almost immediately to my diocese, to fulfill a group of engagements; specifically there were three that were pressing — the dedication of a new, little mission church; the confirmation of a group of adults; and an address to a banquet of salesmen. Thinking about this little triad of duties, I decided that they were a fair sample of what the Church has to do; indeed I looked forward to them with pleasure. But there was also a certain anticipatory sadness about these appointments, for I knew that I should meet again, in each of them, old spirits that are, really, enemies of the Church and of the Gospel.

I would go, for example, to bless a new church; and I would do it with all my heart; but I would know that in large part the building would have been impossible without a spirit that is the enemy of much for which the Church stands — the spirit of the Sect.

I would go confirm a group; and I would rejoice at the apostolic sacrament; but I would also know that to many of them who would receive the Spirit, nothing more would seem to have happened than that, in a rather quaint way, they had 'joined the Episcopal Church.' It would not occur to them that they were part of a supernatural transaction with infinite horizons.

I would go talk to the salesmen after a good dinner; and I would be glad to have the chance to bear witness for the Church and be a loyal partner to the laymen who get us into these things; but I would also know that the framework within which I spoke would be that of the Optional God.

I do not complain because these are the conditions of our ministry. We have far more than the first Christians had. But as we have more, so is more required of us, particularly in our awareness of the corruption even of the best. The interior spirits that bind and weaken the sinews of the Gospel are the most dangerous enemies, far harder to see than the outlines of our task in the post-Christian world.

One is the spirit of the Sect. Another is the loss of the sense of the Supernatural. The third is Optionalism.

Let me identify them a bit more closely. Necessarily I see them against the background of the Episcopal Church; yet I am sure it would not take much imagination to translate them into any other terms. In the womb of every Christian body two spirits wrestle — the Church spirit and the Sect spirit. The Church spirit is generous and inclusive; it is rooted in life, in people and places rather than in ideas and abstractions. Its characteristic locus is the parish, a piece of ground with the people who inhabit it. Michonneau — imaginative and evangelical Roman Catholic though he is — describes it in terms that apply directly to every Church:

Our parish is this entire territory; all those living inside this section are committed to our care, without any exception made because of nationality or immorality or hostility to the clergy. Nothing can free us from the obligation of caring for their souls . . . our parish life should inform the life of all these people; the spiritual life of those who have any . . . their workaday life; their life at home, at rest. That life is made up of the very air that they breathe, the things that occupy them, the joys and sorrows they have known, the influences which play upon them.*

This is the locus of the Church spirit.

Its characteristic expressions are not elaborate catechisms or statements of intellectual convictions and dogmatic detail, but acts, and a community of people. In my own Church, for example, the Book of Common Prayer is just such a characteristic expression. We invite the world to come into our Church, and we subject them to no rigorous examination of the minutiae

* Abbe G. Michonneau, *Revolution in a City Parish*, Newman Press, 1949, p. 11.

of their belief or life, but we say 'Here is the Book. Here are the prayers we say — here are the acts we do together — here is the common life of our fellowship. If you can freely and gladly say these prayers and join in these acts, that is all we ask.'

Even the Creeds themselves, to my way of thinking, are not catechisms. They are our war songs; they are our family saga. We are not individuals who come together because we happen to believe that there is a God; we are the company of those who believe in God, who have staked their lives on the God Whom the Creeds describe. For the Church spirit is not concerned with uniformity but with unity, a vastly different thing. She is quite content to be all ragged at the edges so long as there is a united body at the center. She is, rightly, far more concerned at schism than she is at division of opinion. Indeed, what is the sting of heresy is not conflict of belief but the breaking of the body.

The Sect spirit is the opposite of this. It tends to be exclusive and suspicious. It delights in elaborations of intellectual and moral doctrine. The flood of catechisms in the Reformation period was characteristic — the freezing, and the lace-like elaboration of doctrine, after the exhilarating inventiveness and freedom of the Middle Ages. For myself, I welcome more and more, the older I get, the sober simplicity of the Prayer Book catechism, written at a time when it was very unfashionable to be so sober and simple, with its wonderfully prosaic and matter-of-fact opening, 'What is your name? Who gave it to you?'

It would be wrong to deny that there is much to be grateful for in the Sect spirit. It sharpens questions; it excites loyalty; it dazzles and sparkles in terms of doctrine; it wins allegiance in critical times; it helps to pose questions that require answers. But it is essentially hostile to the Church spirit. Its chief concern seems often to be how best to keep people out of the Kingdom. Its vision of the Church seems often to be not one of a community of people gathered around God and the things of God, but rather of a right-thinking minority within that community, shrinking into doctrinal agreement rather than expanding in life and work.

The Sect spirit is hostile because it looks within rather than without, because it is concerned too much with ideas and not enough with man and the world, because it leads inescapably into absolutes short of God. Inescapably it cuts the nerve of the Church's mission because it concentrates on itself.

It is the spirit that leads people to say they 'believe in the (Episcopal, Baptist, Presbyterian, Roman Catholic or whatever) Church.' There is a sense in which we all do, I suppose, 'believe' in our Churches — yet fundamentally we do not believe in them; we are not baptized into them; we are not ordained as ministers of them; our sacraments are not Episcopalian or Presbyterian or whatever sacraments. The most we hope for our Churches is that they will be faithful companies of the members of Christ's One, Holy, Catholic, and Apostolic Church. Without that reference to the Great

Church, our little bands become sects, filled with people who put their faith in a man-made institution.

And is there anything worse than the dreadful treadmill of a sectarian congregation? The endless fight to raise more money so we can go on another year and raise more money so we can go on . . . This is a paper church, which goes nowhere, which has no dream except to keep its doors open, which has no idea of a new world except a safer one for itself so it can go on and raise more money so it can go on . . . That treadmill, what a curse it is. And what a curse it lays on the minister as on the people, condemned to the endless intellectual drudgery of defensiveness, concerned only to keep the treadmill going and to find enough victims to replace the exhausted, whose sermons are simply justifications of the treadmill, forever defensive, forever apologetic, forever wheedling the world to come in so the treadmill can go on and raise more money so it can go on . . .

I do not know why we have to spend so much time housekeeping in the Church. It is not the vocation of the Church to worry about herself; it is her job to keep her eyes outward, where people are, working and living and dying. That is the spirit of the Church.

The spirit of the Sect has a twin — the loss of the sense of the Supernatural. Indeed it is the ultimate fate of the Sect spirit, to be left to its own devices because it has put its own devices ahead of the overwhelming reality of God. We grow to be like the little group of John's disciples in Ephesus, who looked in wonder

when St. Paul asked them about their confirmation
and stammered, 'Why, we have not so much as heard
that there be any Holy Spirit.' Again to cite my own
communion, the 'gentleman's religion' is our characteristic form of this. Episcopalians are likely to understand that the Prayer Book is the way a gentleman talks
to God (except for a few passages, like the twenty-third
Psalm in the King James Version) for God is a gentleman, too. We like nothing better than the balanced
prose of Elizabethan penitence. We understand that it
is right to say that 'we have left undone those things
which we ought to have done; and we have done those
things which we ought not to have done; and there is
no health in us.' But it would come as something of a
shock to many of us if we thought that God really took
this seriously. One assures one's hostess that one cannot remember when one has had a more pleasant eve-
ning; but it really would be going too far if the hostess
gave us any argument about it. It is the convention of
a gentleman; so is the General Confession. It is the way
the literate and humane man speaks to God.

Another expression is our obsession with history.
People ask an Episcopalian what something means, and
we instantly give them a lecture about how it came
into the Church, and feel that if we can only trace the
history of something we have thereby justified it. I do
not have any quarrel with history; all I am saying is
that often it does not answer people's real questions.
I know why I wear puff sleeves on my rochet, but that
has nothing to do with the apostolic ministry. Yet we

continue in the delusion; we pass on to confirmation classes more miscellaneous information about the history of albs, amices, archdeacons and so on; and it is the purest waste of time I know, for it builds up that strange body of informed ignorance we sometimes call 'churchmanship,' with a hideous emptiness at the very heart of it — people who know all about God and His historic ways but do not know Him.

How all of us professing Christians need to recapture vivid and sharp knowledge of the reality of God. 'Churchmanship' can be diabolic in its power to obscure the supernatural. It can lead people to come to church readily enough, when times are prosperous and life is easy; but when there is pain and doubt, then they go to the witch doctors and the bartenders and the lawyers. They have not so much as heard that there be any Holy Spirit to help them in their need.

These, then, are the hostile spirits — these, and the spirit of Optionalism — which sap our strength from within. It is not so hard, I say again, to see the forms the Church's mission should take. It is hard to fulfill that mission when we are divided within, because we do not understand what we mean when we say the Church is One, Holy, Catholic, and Apostolic. All too often we refute the oneness by our sectarian spirit, we confuse the holiness with tradition and history, and we convert 'Catholic' and 'apostolic' to mean no more than private code words to describe the particular form of sect we prefer.

The forms, the techniques of the Church's mission

are dictated by the society to which we minister. There is no great trick to them; there is no magic in techniques. Little by little, as we reflect on the nature of our society, we see what we should do. The great significance of Abbe Michonneau's book, *Revolution in a City Parish,* is not in his description of the techniques; it is in the extraordinary clarity with which he understands the nature of the Church, and the variegated and confused nature of society. He finds again the age-old function of the parish. He does not pretend it is something magical; it is simply the Church adapting herself to the actual condition of her people.

In our pluralistic society, the parish has a very much more limited usefulness than it does in France. It is necessary for our souls' health that we continue to think in terms of the parish, but it would be delusion to suppose that in any composite American community the texture of the Parisian church could be reproduced.

Our inventiveness will lie in other areas — the rediscovery of the family, for one thing, and of the Church in every man's house. We shall become more and more conscious of the community; and we shall build new communities as cells within industry, within the college. We shall grow more inventive with respect to the ministry itself as we grow more sensitive to the natural groupings of people.

'Penetration' and 'partnership' will describe our mission at every point; and we shall discover as I have discovered for myself the great descriptive power of the Gospel images — the Leaven and the Light.

We shall also discover once more the ambiguities, the confusions of the Church's mission. An optional, professionalized Church is a very neat Church; it knows what is right; it has its paper absolutes clearly before its eyes. But when the Church begins to penetrate society, it becomes involved in painful relativities. It is no longer neat. It is required to take sides. It discovers that its windmills and straw men are not nearly as clear in real life as they are in the pulpit.

This is the hardest part, when enemies turn out sometimes to be friends, when comfortable assumptions about the world, the flesh, and the devil turn out to be quite deceitful. Churchmanship seems to have little relevance to the actual issues; God seems to have had some strange witnesses; and we do not quite know what to do about them. The Church and the Kingdom are confusing to us. We wonder what relationship the two actually bear to one another. Yet we know that in some deep way they are related; and the petty and troublesome relativities of the Church in the world must somehow be brought into some intelligible relationship with the absolutes of the Gospel.

For, despite the ambiguities, in the end it comes to this — that we are the servants of the Kingdom when we are the true servants of the Church. All the confusion we encounter at the superficial levels, all the ambiguities and the unfinished answers and the incomplete relationships of the Church in her mission to the world — all these are reflected in the Gospel; they are even found in the King Himself, and His work.

We have only to ask the old questions again, 'Is the Kingdom present or is it still to come? How do you know if you are in the Kingdom or not? What does Christ mean by the Kingdom being among us?' We have only to ask those uneasy questions again, as I do, against the background of nineteen centuries of the Church's life, to see what a prodigious answer is suggested.

The secret of Church and Kingdom alike are hidden in the doctrine of creation. I suggested in the last chapter that the doctrine of creation is not a doctrine of an act or a series of acts. It is a story of God in His love calling the cosmos out of nothing; implanting and communicating His laws; stage by stage evoking from it a response to Him so that at no level is the creation simply clay in His hands but is alive with His life and is as close to Him and in a sense as large a part of His life as a story written by an earthly writer; at each level giving it such of His purpose and will as it can receive and respond to; moving always toward the sublime end of the perfect response, when in utter freedom and in personal communion, created love will finally answer creating love in the offering of all things to the Eternal Father from whom they came.

It is the end — the free oblation of the Cross — that fulfills and explains and makes right all that has gone before. That is why the Eucharist is part of all life, not just part of religion. That is why the Cross is continuous with all else in creation.

That is why the Kingdom is like leaven in the lump rather than simply the apocalyptic fact at the end of time. That is why the Kingdom is present as well as future. The Kingdom of God is another way of talking about final reality. It is reality pressing in on the creation at every level, giving and evoking as deeply as that level can sustain, moving always toward its ultimate realization in full and free reception and response in the final obedience of the ineffably free will of the Incarnate Lord.

The Kingdom of God is therefore always immediately impending, always pressing through the very veil of Creation itself; yet it is always waiting too, still to be won. In its way, the rock or the flower knows the Kingdom more fully than man does; yet rock and flower and man himself wait for a day when we shall see the Kingdom and the King, face to face.

How this is all so simple in the Gospels. Our Lord walks like a King around this world. He touches it anywhere, and there is truth suddenly there to be seen. He considers the lilies of the field, which in their way know more of the Kingdom than the wise and prudent know — He reaches out to touch the creation everywhere, and the Kingdom is there. The stones themselves would cry out, if they could. The earth, the bread, the clay on a blind man's eyes — reality is making itself known, and the creation is responding to the Word, as best it can, in the dumb obedience of the creature.

He lifts His eyes from the earth to men, and He gravely beholds the men of good will who are not far from the Kingdom. Even those outside the covenant still eat of the crumbs that fall from the Master's table. There is not one God and one truth for them, and another for Israel. 'Many shall come from the East and from the West, from the North and from the South, and shall sit down in the Kingdom.'

For the Kingdom is Reality, and its King is the Word going forth from the Father Who speaks it, a Word to be heard and understood, obeyed and loved everywhere; for without Him was not anything made that was made.

Therefore the Kingdom is one and continuous; and it is present at every time and place, limited only by the freedom of the creation to acknowledge it, to see and obey, to respond and to offer.

At the simplest levels of creation, response is wholly of God's initiative. The rock and the flower praise Him without awareness of alternative. The King reigns and He is obeyed. But as we traverse this multi-leveled creation, we see that there is a movement away from the simple and the unresponsive to the complex and the more responsive, as if God were impatient with the merely obedient, with the merely docile — as if He were reaching for an answer in His terms rather than in the Creation's terms.

Our Lord seems to teach us this in the way He steadily moves from the passive to the personal. At the summit of His teaching, it is not 'the King,' but 'the Father' of Whom He speaks; and it is into the Father's hands that He commends His spirit in the end. A king rules and his subjects obey; a father creates and loves, and his sons come to know and love him back. The story of Creation then is more than a story of clay or of obedience; it is more than even the story of a writer; it is the story of a Father and His children.

The point I am making is that the Kingdom is continuous and universal. We meet the Kingdom everywhere in the long travail of Creation; therefore the question whether it is present or future is, as we come to see, an ambiguous one. It is both. For whatever reality time may have, and the Creation itself, we shall not perfectly see the Kingdom until the end, whatever that is. But at this moment the Kingdom is among us: 'Now is the accepted time.'

St. John saw this most clearly. We sometimes say that there is a 'spiritualized eschatology' in St. John. I dislike the adjective if it suggests an unreal or softened eschatology. There is nothing unreal or soft about the teaching of the Fourth Gospel. St. John saw clearly that there was, at every moment, a kind of intersection of time and eternity; and he saw that the intersection did imply a sort of duality in the mode of the Kingdom, that in some sense it was present and working now, yet in another sense it was still to come.

But the jewel at the heart of the Fourth Gospel is not metaphysics. St. John saw that the heart of this intersection of time and eternity was the point of freedom — that it was fundamentally a moral intersection

rather than simply a metaphysical one. His way of saying what I have stated clumsily is 'We know that we
have passed from death unto life, because we love the
brethren.' That immortal passage from death to life
is seen always and everywhere in the universe. For the
inanimate creature there is one way of passage. For
man there is another and a harder way, the way of
freedom, only perfectly seen in the Cross. But it is the
same passage; and no part of Creation is very far from
it, yet it is always infinitely far from those who do not
freely choose it.

All this I hope is not simply a digression. What I am
saying is that the Church is handicapped in her mission
to the secular world by many things — the spirit of the
sect, the loss of the vivid sense of the supernatural, the
myth of optionalism — and she is supremely handicapped by her confusions and ambiguities in trying to
understand her own nature and the nature of secularism. A post-Christian secularism is a puzzling phenomenon; and it is not as easy as it looks to define the
Church's relation and duty toward it.

My only point now, and it is a point of small com-
fort I must admit, is that the ambiguities in which the
Church finds herself are reflected in the ambiguities of
Creation itself and of the Kingdom. The Church is not
the Kingdom, yet she always approaches the Kingdom
as the end; she is always controlled by the Kingdom
and conforms to it, where she is the Church and not a
sect. Church, Kingdom, and Creation — all alike are
unfinished and show the marks of it, yet to some degree

and in some way are touched and redeemed by eternity at every point. Therefore to ask 'What is the Church's sphere in life, or what is her mission' is really to ask 'What is the Kingdom of God, and where is the Kingdom at work?' It is even to ask 'What is the nature of Creation and how do we understand it?' The Kingdom is continuous with all of life, and so is the Church.

There is a Church of sorts at every level. There is a Church in nature, in the mountains and the forest. The man who tells us that he finds his God and his religion in the wilderness, in nature, is not deceiving himself. He does; the Kingdom is there and the Church is there. The trouble is not that he is deceiving himself about the Church; he is deceiving himself about himself. He has never understood that you cannot go backward in Creation, back to the passive innocence of nature. He has forgotten the angel with the sword of fire who stands at the gateway of innocence and bars his return. There is only one way for man; that is toward conflict, toward choice, toward freedom, toward the Cross, toward free self-giving. The Church of nature is part of the true Church, but it is not where man can find himself.

There is a Church outside the self-conscious Church, the Church of the men of good will who yet stand apart from the historic theology of our tradition. They see the same kingdom we do. Indeed they often see it more clearly than we do. Are they outside the Kingdom and outside the Church because they are outside our company? It is like asking if there are two truths. The

Church of the unbeliever is still the true Church, imperfectly though he may see and understand it.

What of the old Covenant? Again the same answer is suggested. The primitive Christian did not find a new Church. He found something new in the old Church. He saw for the first time what the old Church really meant, and how it was fulfilled. He did not hear a new law; he got behind an old law to what had established it.

The Kingdom is continuous; the Church is continuous; there is one Church, at every level finding its proper mode, until in the Incarnate Word it is fulfilled, and our vision is clear.

Therefore the essence of the Church, like the essence of the Kingdom, is not a law or a definition or a framework of abstract belief. The essence of the Church is an act, an oblation; and it is power given in proportion to the act.

The purpose and meaning of Creation point irresistibly toward an act of offering that will complete the created process. The Church is the locus of that act. The Kingdom is the power-filled realm of those who, with their King, have learned and mastered the secret of offering.

Again I say, how the Gospels illuminate all this. Where do you find Christ's teaching of the Kingdom? It is written in parables, it is summed up in controversies, it is epitomized in the Beatitudes, it is revealed in teaching and healing. Yet we never really come to full understanding of the Kingdom until we go beyond words and behold the Cross itself. While men talk and doubt, He, wordlessly, raises all Creation in His hands and will, and offers it. That act is the foundation stone of the Kingdom. It is not a religion He establishes; it is a way of dealing with life. If we try to make a religion out of it, we lose it.

The Gospels are filled with tentative religions. 'Lord, how oft shall my brother offend against me, and I forgive him? Till seven times?' There is a good sample of liberal religion, that generous approximation. But suddenly we perceive that it has nothing to do with the Kingdom. The Kingdom is the seventy times seven of the life offered rather than of the life managed.

The Pharisee fasted twice in the week and gave tithes of all that he possessed, an exemplary religion. That is precisely the tragedy of the Pharisee. He had too much religion. He was its servant instead of God's son. So it is always in the Gospels — the Kingdom explodes through our words and our approximations, explodes in acts, gleaming ahead of us beyond the words.

As in the Kingdom, so is it in the Church. The heart of the Church is an offering. Creed and Bible and ministry and sacraments all minister to something quite outside of themselves. They are meaningless as ends in themselves. We do not say 'I believe that there is a God,' as if in that passive observation there could be hidden a saving truth. We say 'I believe in God. — I stake my life on God; and I offer my life to Him whom I trust.' The Church is the locus of the universal offering that fulfills Creation and opens the door of the Kingdom. The Church is the Creation, offering and being offered. The Church is the breaking crest of the wave of the universe returning to Him from Whom it comes. The Church is existence itself, fulfilled and being fulfilled in the endless and inexhaustible liturgy of time.

Therefore I think it is an idle question to ask what place the Eucharist has in the life of the Church. If the Eucharist is simply a 'religious' act, if it is simply some kind of cosmic parlor trick the Church has somehow got in possession of, then it has nothing to do with reality. If all that was to be offered was Christ, or the memory of Him, the Eucharist would be no more than a tragic archaeology.

But it is not so; 'Here we offer and present unto Thee, O Lord, ourselves, our souls and bodies' — nay, more, we offer the work of our hands. William Temple reminded us that the real significance of the Offertory lay not in the offering of nature itself but in the offering of nature plus freedom, nature plus work. Bread is a manufactured thing. It is wheat plus the hands and mind and freedom of man. In the Bread, it is as if the universe has come full cycle, and through the pain and fire of the choice of man himself, returns to the Creator in realized love.

Therefore the Eucharist is the Church, and it is the Kingdom, for it is the point at which the offering becomes most vivid and immediate, and where we consciously and freely join in the offering and make it our own. But Eucharist and Church alike point away from themselves. What we see and share so vividly at the altar and in the Liturgy has an inescapable compulsion about it. It will not be a right offering until all work is offered, and the nation and the school and the factory and all mankind themselves. The Eucharist is not a religious act; like the Kingdom and the Church it is continuous with all life. All life comes to its fullness in offering. The Kingdom is offering.

But the final thing to say is that the Kingdom is power. The Gospel is not a Church, or a classroom, or a law court; it is not simply an act of offering: it is the good news of a warfare and a victory already won and continually being won. From the exultation of the Magnificat and the angels' song to the last, magnificent promise, 'Lo, I am with you always . . . ,' the Gospel is at every point a story of victory won, and of power released in the world to those who seek and know and live the truth.

The distinguishing mark of the Kingdom is power. Think of the great climaxes that mark the Gospels — the Temptation, the healings, the Beelzebub controversy, the Mission of the Seventy, — what is central every time is not an abstract truth or a new law alone but a new kind and degree of power to do God's will. 'If I by the finger of God cast out the demons, then, no doubt, the Kingdom has come.' The demons were the same, the good will was the same, the battle was the same. 'By whom do your sons cast them out; let them be your judges.' What had changed was the power to win the victory finally and irrevocably.

The Seventy returned with joy; so does the Church forever return with joy, because through the obedience of the Cross she finds a new access to the very creating and sanctifying power of God Himself.

Now what has this to do with the spirit of this world? It has everything to do with it. The Kingdom and the Church are continuous with all of life — there is one Kingdom and one Church because there is one God and one truth which finds expression at every level of Creation until it comes to its fullest and final realization in the free offering of the Incarnate Lord. From that offering, lived out and fulfilled in the Church and in churchmen, flows the power of God to create and bless, to redeem and make holy, to complete and make right.

Therefore there is no 'religious' sphere set over against a 'secular' one. There is no fraction of truth. God has a warfare with the spirit of the world, but it is like the warfare of sun and shadow; shadows grow and fade with the sun, they would not exist without the sun, and even in the shadow there is a little light.

The world is full of men who are not far from the Kingdom. The Church may curse them, but God does not curse them. What truth they know is His; the impulse that has driven them to find that truth is His; indeed they may be more obedient to Him than the children of light. For I end as I began, with the sober fact that a secular society is Judgment, first of all.

Therefore let the Church seek Judgment, and walk humbly before our God. Let her not forget that what she seeks to be is not an empire but a light, not a judge but leaven in the lump of unredeemed society. Let her give thanks for all truth and for the indomitable purposes of all men of good will. Let her bear her witness, in clearer thought and more consecrated purpose, in company with any who will walk with her. Let her remember always her mission to 'out-think, out-live, and out-die' the pagan world, remembering the promise of her Lord and the power of His Kingdom. Let her hold generous and devoted hands aloft in offering the world to Him from Whom it comes, and unto Whom be glory in the Church by Christ Jesus, world without end.